FISHING FAME!

FISHING FAME!

How to Catch a World-Record Fish

Jeanne Craig

RAGGED MOUNTAIN PRESS / MCGRAW-HILL
CAMDEN, MAINE • NEW YORK • SAN FRANCISCO • WASHINGTON, D.C. • AUCKLAND • BOGOTÁ
CARACAS • LISBON • LONDON • MADRID • MEXICO CITY • MILAN • MONTRÉAL • NEW DELHI
SAN JUAN • SINGAPORE • SYDNEY • TOKYO • TORONTO

Ragged Mountain Press
A Division of The McGraw-Hill Companies

10 9 8 7 6 5 4 3 2 1

Printed in the United States of America.

Library of Congress Cataloging-in-Publication Data
Craig, Jeanne.
Fishing fame: how to catch a world-record fish/Jeanne Craig.
p. cm.
Includes index.
ISBN 0-07-013457-X
1. Fishing. I. Title.
SH441.C69 1999
799.1—dc21 98-51699
CIP

Questions regarding the content of this book should be addressed to
Ragged Mountain Press
P.O. Box 220
Camden, ME 04843
Visit us on the World Wide Web at www.raggedmountainpress.com

Questions regarding the ordering of this book should be addressed to
The McGraw-Hill Companies
Customer Service Department
P.O. Box 547
Blacklick, OH 43004
Retail customers: 1-800-262-4729
Bookstores: 1-800-722-4726

This book is printed on 70-pound Citation
Printed by Quebecor Printing, Fairfield, PA
Production by Dan Kirchoff and Shannon Thomas
Design by Shannon Thomas
All art and photographs courtesy of the International Game Fish Association unless credited otherwise
Edited by Tom McCarthy and D. A. Oliver

CONTENTS

Sidebars

ACKNOWLEDGMENTS

To write *Fishing Fame* I relied on the expertise and authority of talented anglers, respected captains, and veterans in the sportfishing industry. I would like to thank the following people for offering me their valuable time, unique insights, and inimitable enthusiasm: Captain Jim Anson; Stu Apte; Bill Baab; Pam Basco; Marsha Bierman; Del Brown; Jeff Caputo; Jim Chapralis; Allan Cole; Bart Crabb; Jerry Dunaway; Deborah Maddux Dunaway; Jeanne DuVal; William DuVal; Jocelyn Everett; Mike Farrier, president of the Tuna Club of Santa Catalina Island; Mike Fitzgerald; Captain Rick Gaffney; Captain Barkey Garnsey; Tommy Green; Mike Leech, president of the IGFA; Dave Vedder; Porter Hall; George Hommel Jr.; Dan Kadota; Captain Troy Perez; Captain Joe Porcelli; Herbert G. Ratner Jr.; Captain Bob Rocchetta; Terry Rudnik; Steve Schumacher; Stephen Sloan; Captain Frank "Skip" Smith; Captain R. T. Trosset; Raleigh Werking; Captain James Wisner; and Steve Zuckerman. A special thanks to Peter Frederiksen.

INTRODUCTION

To an outsider, fishing is unlike other sports such as football, baseball, and basketball because there are no high-profile celebrities associated with it. For the angling layperson, the personalities most closely linked with stellar achievements in the fishing world are those casting on television broadcasts. Insiders, however, know something more. Anyone who has spent time on the water playing fish knows that many of angling's greatest talents are listed in one place: the record book of the International Game Fish Association (IGFA). Regarded by many as a compilation of the sport's finest feats and most fantastic fish, the IGFA listing, *World Record Game Fishes*, has been called the bible for anglers worldwide. As such, the achievements noted in this book are considered by some to represent the efforts of a superior class of angler, the kind you won't see casting a line on a local river or sharpening hooks in the cockpit of a simple boat. That's one perception, but the fascinating truth is it's not the real picture.

Record anglers are an ambitious and dedicated group, with well-honed instincts, solid angling skills, and a tenacity rivaling that of a stubborn gamefish. But are they really so different from the practiced, knowledgeable anglers with no official claim to fame as yet, fishermen and -women more like you? To find out, I interviewed dozens of record holders. Some of these experts held that they're not different from average anglers. I agree with them, and in this book I'm going to show you why.

Mike Leech, president of the IGFA, estimates that fewer than 1 percent of the more than 35 million anglers in the United States pursue what is regarded as the sport's mightiest challenge. Lack of ambition? You probably can't say that of the people who are committed body and soul to this sport, the avid types who would let their house and yard go to the dogs for just a few more hours out on the water each weekend. The real problem is that many anglers are uninformed: they simply don't know what it takes to break (or make) a record. While the typical angler is aware the IGFA is keeping track of exceptional catches, most are clueless about the marks to beat. As a result, the uneducated angler does one of two things with what could be a record fish: releases it or eats it. Most of the experts say that the real misconception about records is that average anglers don't realize they're eligible to compete and earn a record.

"Every angler has the potential to catch a world-record fish," says Mike Leech. "What they don't always have is the proper mind-set."

Leech has reviewed record applications and has been on the receiving end of the world's most incredible fishing stories since 1983. His conversations with globe-trotting anglers and fanatical fishermen and -women have convinced him that to be successful in the quest for record status, an angler should be keenly focused on the task at hand; then, meticulous preparation must follow.

How do the world's most successful anglers define focus and preparation? That's one of the questions this book will attempt to answer. The following pages are filled with first-hand tips and real-life anecdotes from people who have devoted considerable time, energy, money—and frustration—to the pursuit of world-record fish. For some of these anglers and captains, the accumulation of knowledge has come only after decades of on-the-water training and thousands of lost fish. Is the investment worth it? "You bet!" say these pros. Achieving that first record has a compelling way of igniting an angler's competitive nature, encouraging the search for a second record and making every day of fishing even more of a challenge.

1

PROFILE OF A RECORD ANGLER

Do You Have The Traits of a World-Class Angler?

What Are World Records?

The IGFA was founded in 1939 by Michael Lerner to establish ethical angling regulations and to serve as a central processing center for world-record catch data. Since its inception, the IGFA has set the standard by which sport fish may be caught, and today the organization maintains records internationally for over 600 types of fish.

Records are broken down into different categories. All-tackle records are kept for the heaviest fish of a species caught by an angler in any line class up to 130 pounds (60 kg). In addition, line-class categories are kept according to the strength of the line, from 2-pound up to 130-pound (1 to 60 kg) test. Although the IGFA has a strong saltwater history, it documents records for both saltwater and freshwater game. In salt water, line-class categories are separate for men and women. This nonprofit organization also documents fly-rod records for men and women separately, according to tippet strength, and maintains a relatively new category for junior anglers. The IGFA defines the tippet as the smallest or lightest portion of the leader; record categories range from 2-pound up to 20-pound (1 to 10 kg). In addition, the IGFA book recognizes outstanding angling feats, such as 20-to-1 Club catches—20 or more pounds of fish for each 1 pound of line test.

Records are published in *World Record Game Fishes*, which you can find in your

1996 Edition
World Record Game Fishes
Freshwater, Saltwater, and Fly Fishing
PUBLISHED BY THE INTERNATIONAL GAME FISH ASSOCIATION
1995
World Record Game Fishes
—1997 World Record Game Fishes
Freshwater, Saltwater, and Fly Fishing
PUBLISHED BY THE INTERNATIONAL GAME FISH ASSOCIATION
1998 EDITION
World Record Game Fishes

The bible for any angler seeking a record, World Record Game Fishes *from the International Game Fish Association is updated annually.*

"Fighting that tuna was as physically exhausting as giving birth."

—Jocelyn Everett, 5+ records

local library or purchase from the IGFA (see the resources section of this book). If you're serious about acquiring a record, this annual publication is invaluable.

What do records mean to anglers? For many, an IGFA record is a mark by which a standard of excellence is achieved. For instance, giant bluefin tuna anglers consider Ken Fraser's 1,496-pounder (679 kg) caught on 130-pound line (60 kg) at Auld's Cove, Nova Scotia, in 1979 to be the benchmark by which other giant bluefins are measured.

Ken Fraser's 1979 all-tackle bluefin tuna record of 1,496 pounds (679 kg) is the standard by which other tuna anglers measure their accomplishments.

The IGFA is not the only record-keeping agency in existence. Many states keep their own records, as do some private fishing clubs and national organizations such as the National Freshwater Fishing Hall of Fame. But most anglers consider the IGFA to be the premier source.

People who pursue these records see them as a measure of angling prowess and a pinnacle of achievement. Because you're competing against people around the world, an IGFA record can provide you with a broader measure of how good you are.

Yet in the entire world, there are probably only 50 truly outstanding anglers. Most of these people gradually made the transition from amateur to world-class angler. How did they do it? What qualities, talents and characteristics make the leap possible?

Perseverance

Hard work and perseverance are key, says Raleigh Werking, a 51-year-old angler with over 25 records to his name, including a 39½ pound (17.91 kg) red drum caught on 4-pound (2 kg) line test with Captain Shawn Foster in Cocoa Beach. This Hillsboro Beach, Florida, resident targets records by fishing on charter boats locally and abroad, often with the assistance of some of the sport's most well-respected captains. "There were many trips when I got zip," he says. "And many times I've gone five or six hours on a fish. But I chose to be a light-tackle angler, so I guess I'm not that smart to begin with."

Werking's perseverance helped him cast his way into the books time and again—his 37-pound, 9-ounce (17.03

Raleigh Werking maintains that perseverance and dedication are two essential character traits of a record angler. His tenacity has captured him over 25 records, including this 44-pound, 12-ounce (20.32 kg) Chinook salmon that he took on 2-pound test (1 kg). (Courtesy Raleigh Werking)

kg) chinook salmon caught on 2-pound (1 kg) test was the first 20-to-1 chinook ever caught. Tenacity and a healthy dose of confidence have been keys to his success. Werking discovered this winning combination in 1996, the year he was pressing hard for more records. "I was really trying to make it happen," he says. "I went to Alaska, where I was targeting salmon over the course of 18- to 20-hour days, but the action wasn't very good." So he coupled his salmon attempts with trips to Cocoa Beach, Florida, where he focused on the big red drum that are often spotted swimming near the tattered hems of mangroves. In addition, he made a trip to Panama, where he has had good luck with ultralight line on the healthy numbers of animated sailfish that split the surface of the Pacific ocean with their long, slim bills. Yet for all his tenacity, not a single fish caught was worthy of IGFA scrutiny. "I decided I had to change my attitude," says Werking. "In 1997, I made a decision to take it easy and stop driving my wife crazy."

That's when he got a call from Sue Cocking, outdoor editor of the *Miami Herald*, who gave him a hot tip about a headboat captain in Miami who was putting anglers onto big African Pompano. Werking had never fished for this species before, but despite the lack of experience, he landed a 36-pound (16.32 kg) fish on 6-pound (3 kg) line and took a record. That was just the beginning. In 1997, Werking had one of his best years, with a total of nine records.

The moral?

"Don't give up," he says. "And never underestimate yourself." His résumé is proof. Werking grew up in Maryland catch-

"There were many trips when I got zip. And many times I've gone five or six hours on a fish. But I chose to be a light-tackle angler, so I guess I'm not that smart to begin with. . . . Don't give up, and never underestimate yourself."

—Raleigh Werking, 25+ records

Birth of a Record Keeper

TODAY, ANGLERS WHO make extraordinary catches can be rewarded with a world record from the International Game Fish Association (IGFA). But there was a time when that honor wasn't available.

Until 1939, various institutions and publications used to keep what they called "world-record charts," but they were vague, inaccurate lists. Some of the entries were fish that had been harpooned and shot, not caught on rod and reel. Others were fish that had been dragged to boatside after sharks had torn away half of their flesh, and the weights given were only guesses about what the scales might have registered if the sharks hadn't already dined. Certain clubs—notably in Florida, Australia, Great Britain, and California—had exacting rules for sea fishing and a membership of anglers who were true sportsmen, but these clubs were rare.

In 1939, while in Australia, the late Michael Lerner, founder of the Lerner Department stores and a devoted billfisherman, debated these matters with the late Clive Firth, a noted Australian angler. Firth suggested that one rule-making body should be U.S.-based because of threatening war in Europe and Asia. Lerner agreed and eventually underwrote the expenses for the establishment of what would become the IGFA.

Lerner wasn't a casual angler who took big fish without any interest in the larger implications of the sport. In fact, this angler underwrote seven scientific expeditions of the American Museum of Natural History and founded the Lerner Marine Laboratory in Bimini, Bahamas. Catching the biggest fish wasn't the priority for this angler. In *Profiles in Saltwater Angling*, George Reiger, former editor of *Field & Stream*, tells the story of the time Lerner caught one of the largest mako sharks ever brought into Bimini. Yet it wasn't the size of the fish that impressed Lerner. Rather, it was the fact that inside that shark was a small broadbill swordfish—the first indication the world had that there was a spawning area for this species somewhere in the western Atlantic.

From the beginning, the IGFA has had a strong interest in serving marine science, and that commitment has continued. It's in this spirit that the organization exists today.

In the beginning, the rule-making body of the IGFA was made up of offshore anglers known for their skill and fairness, ichthyologists and other scientists, and fishermen like Van Campen Heilner and the late Ernest Hemingway, who had fished almost everywhere and written on the subject. (Years later, this Pulitzer prize–winning author became an officer of the IGFA.)

The goal of the IGFA was to supply the rules for standard tackle and fair fishing methods to competitive anglers worldwide. In its formative years, the organization admitted as members anglers from established fishing clubs. Today, however, IGFA accepts individual memberships.

In addition to members, the IGFA has "representatives," volunteers who provide members with details on record catches and investigate any questions that arise about a record claim. If information about a catch is insufficient or confusing—for instance, if a fish seems too large for the type of tackle that was used—a local representative may turn up at the scene to investigate.

In any competition, there will be people who cheat, and some anglers *(continued on next page)*

Birth of a Record Keeper

continued from page 4

and captains complain that this is too easy to do when pursuing a world-record fish according to IGFA rules. But since the organization's founding, the IGFA has always relied on the integrity of the angler, since it can't place an inspector in every boat and on every dock and beach.

The IGFA maintains that most anglers are honest people. For those who are not, there are procedures in place that discourage cheating. For instance, expert eyes scan the photographs and read the affidavits submitted with each record application; scientists and veteran anglers review these documents. Of course, anglers who want to cheat generally wind up trying to do so in front of anglers who are more honest sportspeople, those who might spread the word about a questionable application. In the end, an irritated, honest angler could write the IGFA and suggest an investigation be made about a particular application.

ing perch in a pond. Today, he's regarded as one of the most diversified anglers in the country, a unique breed who's at ease casting in locales from Hatteras to Alaska and ports abroad. That flexibility is part of the reason he's so successful today.

"Most of Raleigh's records are very difficult to beat," says Leech. "But he's earned every one of them because he did his homework."

Pure, Dumb Luck

Methodical preparation is everything, say the anglers who've learned the hard way. As you'll discover in the following chapters, preparation encompasses everything from developing an intimate knowledge of equipment to devoting time and thought to the thorough study of a particular species. That's the basic component of fishing success for the people who've had an exceptional amount of it. Yet ironically, many of the anglers who make the pursuit of records a priority, even those who define themselves as obsessed and intense today, say they caught the first one by accident.

Herbert G. Ratner Jr. was 43 years old when he got his name into the IGFA record book for the first time. When he made that record catch, Ratner had never even heard of the IGFA, and in fact he didn't know his catch was exceptional until a stranger walking the dock told him so.

A native of Greensburg, Pennsylvania, Ratner had grown up freshwater fishing in rivers with "big, long Indian names," but he developed an appreciation for saltwater as he

> *What does it take to catch a record fish? "Hunger, obsessiveness, and intensity—the same qualities you need to excel in any sport or in any business, for that matter."*
>
> —Herbert G. Ratner Jr., 60+ records

Herb Ratner has earned more than 60 records since he started targeting trophy fish, yet this 42½-pound (19.27 kg) tarpon caught on 2-pound (1 kg) line test in Florida in 1986 is one of the records he's most proud of. (Courtesy Herb Ratner)

grew older. He caught mostly amberjack and dolphin in his twenties, but when he turned 35 and his children were more independent, this well-to-do entrepreneur decided to devote more energy to more serious fishing. Having recently sold his real estate businesses, Ratner had the time to travel to the exotic fishing destinations he'd read about in magazines. His passion for travel was matched by the desire to catch the glamour fish: marlin, sailfish, swordfish, and tuna, among others. He toured some of the world's most legendary fishing grounds, catching his first sailfish in Stuart, Florida, and his first blue marlin off Walker's Cay in the Bahamas. He trolled lines for black marlin off Pinas Bay, Panama, fought makos off Cape May, and cruised north to Nova Scotia to hunt bluefin. He was averaging 60 days of fishing a year, always with charter crews, since he didn't own a boat. With the help of these professional guides, he was fine-tuning his heavy-tackle skills.

When he boarded a center console boat in Key West in 1982 and the captain, Jim Goodacre, handed him a reel with 12-pound (6 kg) test, Ratner's jaw dropped. At the time, his idea of light tackle was 50-pound (24 kg) test. Nevertheless, they went wreck fishing for cobia that day. When an 86-pounder (39 kg) came up on Ratner's line, it was the largest fish of this kind he'd ever seen, as well as his first experience fishing around a wreck. With a lot of coaching from the captain, Ratner was able to keep the fish from reaching the wreck and breaking the delicate line. Eventually, he boated it. "Talk about pure, dumb luck," he says. But his luck got better when a larger cobia took his bait. "A cobia takes long, determined runs, shaking its head the whole way," says Ratner. "But I managed to turn him before he got into the wreck and broke his will on the first run. You can do that on some fish."

They brought the fish back to the dock, where it weighed in at 98 pounds (44.45 kg). Ratner was preparing to transport this massive fish to a taxidermist when a stranger told him the cobia could qualify as a record. "I couldn't sleep that night," says Ratner. "I never dreamed I could be a world champion of a sport I loved. I felt fantastic, and I believed I didn't need to achieve anything else to be happy. That attitude lasted until the next morning, when I sobered up."

The cobia, which still stands today as the mark to beat on 12-pound (6 kg) test, was the accidental record that motivated Ratner to make fishing for records his life's passion. "I'm a perfectionist by nature. I never give up. I don't think I'm brilliant, but I'm tenacious." Thanks to persistence, Ratner now has over 60 records to his credit. When I asked him which qualities are essential to be that good, he replied: "Hunger, obsessiveness, and intensity—the same qualities you need to excel in any sport or in any business, for that matter."

Commitment

For truly obsessed record anglers, dedication is a key to success. Steve Schumacher is setting one of the best examples of that today. This 45-year-old insurance entrepreneur has at least one record to his credit, but his primary goals include boating the first 2,000-pound (907.18 kg) marlin and securing a 130-pound (60 kg) line class or all-tackle record for a blue or black marlin. Those are lofty ambitions, when you consider the largest marlin in IGFA record history is Alfred Glassel's 1,560 pound (707.61 kg) black. Schumacher's strategy? He fishes 80 to 100 days a year, either aboard his boat, the *Kila Kila* captained by Randy Parker, or abroad. And he's been traveling in pursuit of a record for 12 years.

"I was born in Iowa, and I remember watching Curt Gowdy on *The American Sportsman* when I was a boy. I'd see those marlin jump and I would dream about a fish that could take all my line, as fish did in the books and magazines I read." In 1986, Schumacher traveled to Hawaii, where he went fishing on a charter boat. That day, he hooked a fish estimated at over 700 pounds (315 kg). "It took the line and went. It cleaned a spool of 130-pound [60 kg] line."

> *"Until you weigh 'em, they don't mean a thing."*
>
> —Steve Schumacher, 1,000 marlin catches

That fish helped put him on a quest for records. But record fishing isn't always easy. You'll pay your dues, says Schumacher, who remembers the marlin he had on the line for 23 hours before it broke off. He estimates it weighed more than 1,500 pounds (680.38 kg), "but it's just a fish story," he says, dismissing his own catch. "Until you weigh 'em, they don't mean a thing."

His advice to those who are angling for a record: be mentally prepared. "During a fight, some anglers exert too much energy too early. You have to think like a pro boxer, who's mentally prepared for 12 rounds. And be prepared to deal with the setbacks. Life doesn't always give you the lucky ones."

Be a Good Listener

What makes a world-class angler? Captain Tred Barta, an outdoor writer and record holder, was asked that question in an interview published in *Marlin* magazine. When the author asked him if he thought you could pull someone off the street and turn them into an exceptional offshore angler, his response was "yes."

"A world-class angler listens to and follows instructions to the letter." He used record holder Pam Basco as an example. "She caught six sailfish on 4-pound [2 kg] test fishing with me one winter day off Palm Beach all because she listened to instructions and responded accordingly. To me, that's the essence of being a world-class angler. Can you make one from scratch? A couple of newcomers, who, after hiring the best crews, in a very short time have come from nowhere to prominence, winning tournaments and setting world records. So obviously, it's possible. And more than money, it takes enthusiasm and fervor to be the best."

Why Fish for Records?

Dedication is what makes the best anglers, but what makes these anglers so dedicated? What's the big deal about catching a record fish, anyway? You hear embellished talk about the thrill of catching a fish that runs like a freight train. Less poetic anglers contend records are also about earning respect and stroking the ego. But Jerry Dunaway—who became the media's darling in the 1980s when he revealed his plans to troll the globe for billfish records aboard a 110-foot (33.5 meter) mothership—summed it up for many of his peers when he said: "Fishing is my mountain. Some people run marathons, some climb mountains. I want to do what I'm good at, and that's fishing."

Dunaway isn't the only one who believes the reward for time spent pursuing records is well worth the effort. It seems a record meant just as much to Howard L. (Rip) Collins. In 1992, this angler caught a 40-pound, 4-ounce (18.25 kg) brown trout in Heber Springs, Arkansas. That fish became the all-tackle record for the species, and it stands as the mark to beat today. Collins often told family and friends that the trout was his life's achievement. To prove it, he was buried with a replica of that amazing catch when he died a few years later.

Many anglers would give their casting arm to claim bragging rights to a fish like Collins's trout. After all, one of the fulfilling rewards of record fishing has to be the fame that comes with a noteworthy catch. Celebrity is one reason anglers worldwide are fascinated and obsessed with the extraordinary marks that are tough to beat, including the oldest all-tackle record, a 4-pound, 3-ounce (1.91 kg) yellow perch caught in 1865, and the heaviest all-tackle record, a 2,664-pound (1,208.38 kg) white shark landed on 130-pound (60 kg) line class in 1959 by Alfred Dean.

Those are the glamour records, but if you're really serious about getting your name in *World Record Game*

Howard L. "Rip" Collins said his all-tackle record 40-pound, 4-ounce (18.25 kg) brown trout, caught in Arkansas, was his life's achievement.

Fishes, take tips from the pros. You'll find a variety of how-to advice in the pages that follow, along with references to many great catches. For those noteworthy fish that are missed, please accept my apologies. I only wish I had space to mention them all.

The combined experience of the anglers listed in the IGFA book—as well as the captains and crews who helped to get them there—could possibly teach you more about nailing a trophy fish than you can teach yourself in a lifetime. Their advice: start with simple goals and don't forget to have fun.

Captain Kelly Everett of Kona, Hawaii, with his wife Jocelyn Everett and Kelly's world-record blue marlin, caught on 30-pound (15 kg) line test. (Courtesy of Jocelyn Everett, © James Sloan)

The Danger Element

Record fishing has an allure of danger, too, which can be compelling for a certain type of person. Yet some of the more intriguing anglers confront the risk with a James Bond–like coolness. Stewart Campbell, a Houston-based businessman who devotes most of his spare time to light-tackle fishing in waters best known for high volumes of billfish, once fought a 200-pound (90.71 kg) billfish that jumped into the boat, where it thrashed around more violently than a teenager in a mosh pit. So what did Campbell and his crew do? "We tagged it," says Campbell's captain, Barkey Garnsey, "opened the transom door, and kicked it out. No problem."

Alfred Glassel, Marlin Record Holder

ALFRED GLASSEL, who fished from such a young age that one of his earliest memories was of being pulled off a dock into a lake by his first fish, grew up to become a famous and well-respected angler. This Louisiana native turned Texas businessman caught the largest marlin of any species. His 1,560-pound (707.61 kg) black was taken on 130-pound (60 kg) test in 1953, yet this colossal catch still stands as the all-tackle record.

It was caught in Cabo Blanco, Peru, a small town best known as the location of the Cabo Blanco Club, an exclusive fishing fraternity founded in 1951 by saltwater angler S. Kip Farrington. The club—which had an upscale membership fee of a cool $10,000—counted only about two dozen anglers as members, but all shared a passion for big marlin, which were often dining in the area on mackerel or plump, 3-foot (1 m) squids that schooled on the ocean's surface. Glassel was an early member, and he traveled to this distant port to battle behemoth fish from one of the club's three motorcruisers. Marlin, aristocrats of the saltwater gamefishes, would challenge his skills and strain his tackle as they leaped from the water and hung momentarily stark against the sky, water spewing from their glistening backs, fins spread in defiant rage.

Some people would try to belittle the efforts of Glassel and the marlin anglers at the Cabo Blanco Club. George Weller's 1956 article in *Sports Illustrated* (March 19) referenced how even novices got lucky there. "Ted Williams, while ruminating on his divorce from his wife and temporarily baseball, flew down in December 1954 and casually took a 1,235-pound [564.71 kg] marlin," wrote Weller. "A tall girl named Kimberly Wiss, who works in New York for a public relations firm, took a 1,525-pounder [691.72 kg] after an 80-minute battle."

Sure, there are anglers who get lucky on marlin, but if that happens, it does so only once. Glassel proved he knew a (continued on next page)

Alfred Glassel's 1,560-pound (707.6 kg) black marlin, caught on 130-pound (60 kg) line test in Peru is one of the most famous fish in history. The record has been standing since 1953.

Alfred Glassel, Marlin Record Holder

continued from page 10

lot about handling big fish with a series of phenomenal catches.

Prior to his all-tackle record, he was the first to boat a black marlin over 1,000 pounds (453.59 kg), breaking Captain Laurie Mitchell's record for a 976-pound (442.70 kg) black immortalized in Zane Grey's *Tales of an Angler's El Dorado*. Then, in 1952, he caught a 1,025-pounder (464.92 kg) and 1,090-pounder (494.41 kg) within one month. That flurry of activity was no accident. It proved that Glassel pursued his fish with the same dogged determination characteristic of the most successful record-seeking anglers today.

His famous marlin is just one contribution Glassel made to sportfishing. This angler also gave his time and money to marine science; among his efforts, he led a Yale University expedition that delivered over 8 tons of new forms of sea life to the institution. However, most of us will remember him for the fantastic fish he caught. His record remains the ultimate measure of the sport for serious marlin fishermen.

Think Positively

Cynics say some records just cannot be beaten: some of the all-tackle trophies, for instance, are so tremendous that it would be a miracle to find a fish that size, never mind catch it. That's partially true, but don't let the negative logic sink your hopes. According to the IGFA, roughly 10 percent of existing records change hands each year. In addition, the organization adds new species and line classes every few years, thereby increasing your chances of getting a record fish. Recently the IGFA opened a new fly fishing category for women, who had long been competing with men in a single category.

A stark reality of record fishing, however, is that if you acquire a record, chances are it won't be long before you lose it to someone else. That's part of the game. And to win it, you have to keep playing. But remember the pros' advice: start simple.

"During a fight, some anglers exert too much energy too early. You have to think like a pro boxer, who's mentally prepared for 12 rounds. And be prepared to deal with the setbacks. Life doesn't always give you the lucky ones."

—Steve Schumacher

Stephen Sloan is a New York real estate and marine developer who has been fishing for 25 years and has about 44 trophy fish to his credit, including an old record for an 862-pound (390.99 kg) black marlin that he caught on 30-pound (15 kg) test. Yet among his reputable catches are some less glamorous species, including bonito.

While fishing off Montauk, New York, one day, his boat came alongside a school of these fighting fish. Sloan plucked his IGFA

"You don't have to harpoon a whale to set the world on fire."

—Stephen Sloan, 40+ records

record book from his seabag and consulted the fly rod section under bonito. He did some quick math and figured what he needed to beat the existing mark on 2-pound (1 kg) tippet. "It took me some time, but I got one that weighed 5 pounds, 15 ounces [2.71 kg]." Not a breathtaking fish, but Sloan's experience that day emphasizes an important point: "You don't have to harpoon a whale to set the world on fire."

2

THE IMPORTANCE OF PLAYING BY THE RULES

According to the pros, you need a straightforward strategy in order to catch a record fish. Most veteran captains and anglers with numerous records to their credit contend that a workable approach is to review the IGFA record book to determine which record is attainable for your skills and style. Then find a place where that species exists in large numbers. In many ways, acquiring a record is as simple as getting a lot of bites from fish of the right size. Many experts encourage newcomers to the world of record fishing to target a local species, since it's often easier to be a good angler in your home waters, where you know when and where to fish and what to expect.

Once you've targeted your catch, the next step is to commit time to pursuing the fish. But before you grab your tackle and head for the nearest fishing hole, you'll need to bone up on the rules.

The rules for world-record angling are included in the IGFA's *World Record Game Fishes*. The rules encompass only a few pages of this meaty publication, but an angler cannot underestimate the importance of reading them carefully. These

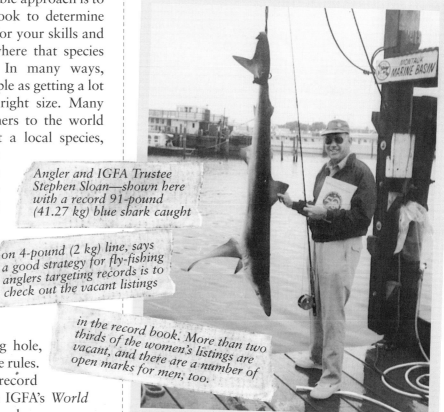

Angler and IGFA Trustee Stephen Sloan—shown here with a record 91-pound (41.27 kg) blue shark caught on 4-pound (2 kg) line, says a good strategy for fly-fishing anglers targeting records is to check out the vacant listings in the record book. More than two thirds of the women's listings are vacant, and there are a number of open marks for men, too.

Don't Leave Home without It

IF YOU'RE SERIOUS about catching a world-record fish, you can increase your chances for success with careful preparation. Begin by packing the following items into your tackle box or accessory bag.

1 **Record Book.** IGFA's *World Record Game Fishes* contains angling rules, which should be studied before you go in search of a trophy fish; pay close attention to tackle specs. This book also lists all records, including the all-tackle, line-class, and tippet-class categories. If you've targeted a certain species for a record, you can memorize the mark to beat. But if you pull in another fish, and it looks exceptionally big, you can compare it to the listing in the book. You may have a winner, but if it doesn't hit the mark, you can release the fish and keep trying.

2 **Record Application Form.** Record contenders must complete a form requiring specific information about the catch. The angler's signature on the completed form, which must be witnessed by a notary, attests to the fact the fish was landed according to IGFA rules. The application must be accompanied by a sample of the line (or tippet) you were fishing with, photographs of your catch, and a cover letter. Applications are available at some tackle shops and fishing clubs; there's also one in *World Record Game Fishes.*

3 **Camera/Film.** Color or black-and-white photographs are submitted with record applications in order to identify the species of fish. Photos must show the full length of the fish, the rod and the reel used to make the catch, and the scale used to weigh it. A photo of the angler with the fish also is required. Try to avoid using cameras that produce instant pictures. In the past, IGFA has had problems identifying fish because the quality of instant shots was poor. If a fish cannot be identified from photos, it's the angler's responsibility to have it examined by an ichthyologist or qualified fisheries biologist.

4 **Tape Measure.** This is an invaluable tool for taking the required measurements of the fish (length and girth). Aside from the fish, the angler also must measure the length of double line, leader, and lure or hook, items which must be submitted with the record claim. Measure off 50 feet (15.25 m) of single line, too, which should be removed from the reel promptly and carefully preserved before presented to IGFA for testing.

5 **Certified Scale.** Record fish must be weighed on scales that have been checked and certified for accuracy by accredited organizations. If you're planning a trip to a remote fishing ground, you should bring your own scales, which should be certified before and after the trip. The fish must be weighed on land and in the presence of one or more witnesses. Names, addresses, and signatures of witnesses and the *(continued on next page)*

Don't Leave Home without It

continued from page 14

weighmaster (the person who weighs the fish if not the angler) must be on the record application.

6 **Cord.** Consider packing cord if you're targeting a billfish. Some anglers tie the bill of a catch when it's landed to prevent weight loss (stomach contents, etc.) when the fish is hung for weighing.

7 **Water/Ice.** To prevent weight loss as well as keep the fish from deteriorating, a fish should be constantly wet or iced down from the time it's boated to the moment it reaches land. This strategy can make or break a record if you have a long cruise to the nearest scale. Remember, in record fishing, every ounce counts.

rules, which have changed little since the IGFA was founded in 1939, promote ethical and sporting practices and are not difficult to follow. In fact, many anglers say the regulations make fishing for sport more challenging and ultimately more fun; even skilled anglers who don't fish for records say they abide by these regulations, since the rules encourage better preparation and can help anyone become a better angler.

However, some anglers don't realize that the IGFA has little tolerance for sloppiness. To prove it, the organization says that, of the world-record applications turned down each year, the majority are rejected for failure to comply with the rules. In more than 15 years of reviewing applications, Mike Leech says he sees the same mistakes made over and over again. Avoid the common stumbling blocks, he advises, and you'll increase your chances for catching a trophy fish.

"To catch a record, you have to know what's possible. . . . It's not difficult to catch a record, but it can be tough to make yourself aware of what's open."

—Jeanne DuVal, 50+ records

Fight Your Own Fish

In November 1988, Jodie Daniels, a novice angler from Alaska, landed a 1,207-pound (547.48 kg) mako shark on 130-pound (60 kg) line while fishing 3 miles (5 km) off Hawaii's Honokohau Harbor aboard *Hustler*, a 32-foot (9.76 m) charter boat. For three hours, Daniels fought the largest mako ever caught on hook and line—the all-tackle record at the time was 1,115 pounds (505.76 kg). But the amazing fish and tenacious angler never made it into the record book. Daniels lost her shot at a title moments after the hit, when a deckhand passed the heavy rod and reel outfit to her as she sat in the fighting chair.

Daniels's mistake was that the IGFA will not consider a record application if any person other than the angler handles the rod at

> *"Fishing is my mountain. Some people run marathons, some climb mountains. I want to do what I'm good at, and that's fishing."*
>
> —Jerry Dunaway, entrepreneur and multiple record holder

any time during the fight. This rule requires the angler to hook, fight, and land the fish without help or assistance. This rule raises an issue for anglers who plan to charter boats in distant locales. Before you book a charter, make sure the crew knows how you want to play the game. If you're shooting for a record, let the team know it before the fish hits. After all, it's not uncommon for a crew to assist an angler in the hope that the charter guest will catch a lot of fish, enjoy the experience, and book the boat again. Also, be aware that, in some locations, captains and mates are not always aware of the IGFA or the rules. For that reason, assess a crew's record fishing knowledge before you select a boat. One way to do that is to contact record-seeking anglers who have fished with the crew in the past. Discuss the crew's qualifications before you book a charter.

The no-assist rule has long been tripping up anglers in search of records, as well as those participating in fishing tournaments based on IGFA regulations. Knowing this, some crews will go to an extreme to avoid breaking the rule. Mike Leech recalls one instance that occurred during a tournament. He was aboard a top game boat as an observer, and he realized his presence was a little unnerving for the crew working the cockpit. This was driven home to him when the angler, a woman, slipped and fell on the cockpit sole while fighting a fish. Yet the crew was so eager to abide by the letter of the IGFA law that not one person stepped forward to help the woman up. Says Leech: "They didn't know if they could touch her while she was holding the reel."

Some record-hunters are so obsessed with the technicalities of IGFA regulations that they've let some remarkable fish go for minor infractions.

According to IGFA representative and author-angler Captain Rick Gaffney of Kona, Hawaii, these anglers are perfectionists, and among the breed is Steve Zuckerman. This land developer and attorney from California is one of the world's most skilled light-tackle anglers. He has set several world records, achieved impressive tournament wins, and was even named Australia's Angler of the Year. No stranger to the IGFA rule book, he's well aware that the no-assist rule says a catch can be disqualified if a person other than the angler touches any part of the rod, reel, or line during the fight. He was thinking about that the day he had a potential world-record blue marlin hooked up on line under 20-pound (10 kg) test. After a skillful fight, he'd brought the fish to the transom and then did what all good light-tackle anglers do. He stepped back to bring the leader closer to the wireman's grasp. That's when the fish surged and the rod bent. In that moment, Zuckerman saw the line rub the shoulder of the wireman. Zuckerman insisted the fish not be submitted as a record, even after the wireman said he never felt the line. "True sporting anglers interpret the rules strictly," says Gaffney.

> *"True sporting anglers interpret the rules strictly."*
>
> —Captain Rick Gaffney, Kona, Hawaii

Know Your Line

If you ever visit the IGFA headquarters in Florida, make sure you get a look at the device anglers refer to as the "heartbreaker." The purpose of the Instron machine, as it's really called, is to test the line samples sent with each record application. (Every line class submission must include at least 10 feet [3 m] of the actual line that caught the fish.) The highly calibrated Instron will test a line sample five times; the results are averaged to determine the breaking strength of the line. Unfortunately, line isn't always what it's rated to be.

One of the most common problems for record-seeking anglers is not knowing their line. Very often, says Leech, line "overtests." For example, say a male angler submits a record application for a Pacific halibut 1 pound (0.45 kg) over the record for the 16-pound (8 kg) line class. IGFA tests the line's breaking strength at 18 pounds (8.16 kg). That means that the fish now qualifies for the next largest line-class category, which is 20 pounds (10 kg). That record, however, is for a halibut 76 pounds (34.47 kg) heavier than the angler's application. Not knowing the strength of your line could cost you the record by pushing you into the next line-class category.

On line regulations, the IGFA is strict, but they give you a few breaks. For example, on 16-pound (8 kg) line, they'll allow a breaking strength up to 17.6 pounds (7.98 kg). And if the line overtests when dry, they'll soak it for two hours and test it again. This procedure can increase breaking strength by up to 10 percent, although percentage varies with the type of line.

To avoid problems with overtesting, experts recommend using tournament-grade line, which many line manufacturers offer today. Chances are it won't overtest the way some regular lines sometimes do, but there are no guarantees. More than one angler has learned the hard way that just because the box says 12-pound (6 kg) line on the outside, doesn't mean it's 12 on the inside.

Albia Dugger discusses exactly this point in "Going to Extremes" (*Sport Fishing*, April 1996). When record-fishing with ultralight lines was just becoming trendy with big-game aficionados in the early 1990s, the editors of *Sport Fishing* tested 76 different ultra-

Anglers call this device the "heartbreaker," but it's better known as the Instron machine, a highly calibrated device that tests the strength of fishing line.

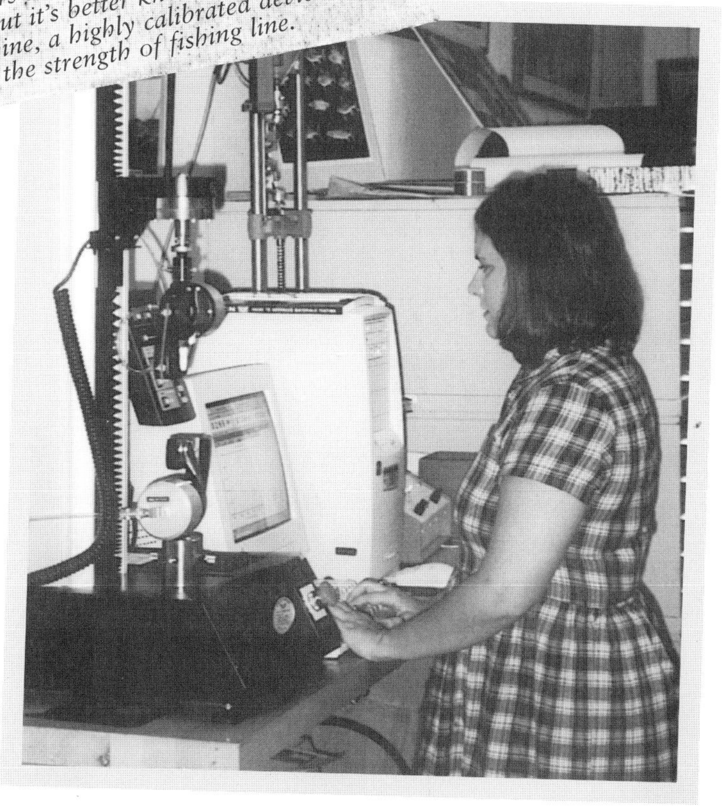

Weighting Game

MANY TROPHY-SEEKING captains and anglers make it their business to become expert estimators on the weight of fish. So equipped, they can determine if the fish is eligible for a record. If it is not, the decision to release is made immediately. Following is one simple method the pros use to calculate the size of a catch.

Measure the length and girth of the fish, then square the girth, multiply it by the length, and divide by 800. This will give you the approximate weight of a fish with a cylindrical body shape. For long, thin fish such as barracuda or king mackerel, divide by 900 instead of 800. A soft tailor's measuring tape is a good choice for measuring fish. Another method some experts recommend is to make a measuring tool by tying a length of parachute cord to a snap swivel and marking the cord every 12 inches (or 10 cm). When the fish is alongside the boat, snap the swivel around the leader and let the cord slide down to the nose of the fish. Now you can eyeball the length as the cord streams alongside the fish's body. Unclip the cord and use it to measure the girth.

light lines to find out how much brands and labels vary in breaking strength and stretch. The answer? A lot.

Of the 30 6-pound (3 kg) lines tested, only 15 averaged within the IGFA requirement of 6.6 pounds (2.99 kg) or less when wet tested, and 15 tested heavier, 4 going well into the 10-pound (4.53 kg) range. As for the 4-pound (2 kg) line, 11 of the 25 tested would have met the IGFA wet-test requirement of 4.4 pounds (1.99 kg) or less; 10 wet-tested over 5 pounds (2.26 kg).

The results emphasize an important fact for record anglers: You must be careful not only to select a line that will break within IGFA limits, but to actually test each spool used. This is particularly true if you're selecting light lines; at light weights, minute variations among spools or batches can mean the difference between approval and rejection of a record. Try to choose a line that wet-tests as close as possible to the breaking limit without going over it.

To do that, professional anglers and captains recommend that you contact fishing clubs—many have certified line-testing machines. Or, you can send line samples to the IGFA, which tests samples for members. High-quality lines show minimal diameter variations throughout a spool. If you consistently use a particular brand with a known breaking strength, buy a good micrometer and measure the line diameter on each spool before you buy it.

Weigh and Release

Contrary to what some people believe, record fishing is not about killing a lot of fish. Granted, the rules require that a record fish be weighed, and for very large or unmanageable species such as marlin or shark, that often means boating the fish and bringing it back to the dock. But don't overlook the fact that many record fish are released today; in fact, some professionals are becoming famous for their conservation efforts on the record-fishing front. Captain Ralph Delph, who runs the *Vitamin Sea* out of Key West, Florida, is one such pioneer. This charter captain has assisted in the capture of over 100 records, and he's lauded for his efforts to weigh fish alive and then release them.

In addition, the IGFA honors outstanding anglers who choose to release fish. In 1992, angler Marsha Bierman, who helped pioneer the use of short rods offshore for billfish and tuna and advocates a no-kill policy, was one of five people selected to receive IGFA's first annual conservation

Contrary to what some anglers think, fish can be caught and released and still qualify for record status. This 6-pound, 8 ounce (2.94 kg) bonefish caught by Susanne Gill (shown here with her captain) was weighed on land according to IGFA rules and then was revived and finally released.

award. It was presented in lieu of the official world record she may have been eligible for if she had killed two fish. One was a Pacific blue marlin she had caught on 50-pound (24 kg) stand-up tackle that was estimated at just under 1,300 pounds (589.66 kg). The other, caught a year later while Bierman was fishing off the Great Barrier Reef in Australia, was a black marlin estimated at over 1,100 pounds (498.94 kg). Both fish were tagged and released, so weights weren't verified. Says Bierman: "I fish against myself. I don't need a scale to measure my accomplishments."

Not all anglers share her philosophy, though. Many like to play by the rules, which includes weighing a catch. Sounds easy, right? Guess again. Many anglers make simple mistakes and disqualify sensational fish.

> *"[The 1973 bass] catch gave hope to a lot of anglers who wanted to be the proud owners of the record, and it almost started a stampede to southern California much like the Gold Rush days."*
>
> —Bart Crabb, bass expert

On March 1, 1997, Paul Duclos of Santa Rosa, California, was fishing 74-acre (30 hectare) Spring Lake near his home. Duclos is an avid trophy bass fisherman. On that day, he was throwing a massive, 6.7-ounce (0.188 kg) Castaic Trout lure when he landed the biggest largemouth he'd ever seen, and he already had a 15-pounder (6.80 kg) to his credit.

As author Jim Mathews described in an *Outdoor Life* article (June/July 1997), Duclos called a nearby outdoor shop and asked the owner to bring a certified scale to the dock. Since the owner was alone and couldn't leave the shop, he had to refuse. Duclos then called his wife, Shelly, and asked her to come down to the lake and to bring their scale—the bathroom scale, with its big dial. There on the dock he weighed himself—180 pounds (81.64 kg). Then he gently lifted the fish out of the water and weighed himself with the bass—204 pounds (92.53 kg).

Even casual bass fishermen and women know that the world record is George Perry's 22-pound, 4-ounce (10.09 kg) bass caught in Lake Montgomery, Georgia, in 1932 (see chapter 6). If Duclos's fish was really 24 pounds (10.88 kg), he had just shattered the existing record by 2 pounds (0.90 kg). (According to IGFA rules, a record under 25 pounds [11 kg] must be broken by at least 2 ounces [0.05625 kg].) But because Duclos prefers to catch and release, he snapped a few photos of the fish with a witness; then he watched as the huge, egg-laden largemouth swam away.

Although Duclos told Mathews that having a record isn't very important to him, he eventually submitted the phenomenal fish for IGFA consideration. But the IGFA had never approved a fish weighed on a bathroom scale, and because this was a very important record, they examined Duclos's application very carefully. There were a few problems: the scale wasn't certified by a recognized organization, and Duclos hadn't measured the fish—length is required on the record application. Eventually, the record was denied. Although it's permissible for an angler to use his own scale, that provision exists only if the scale is certified before and after the fish is weighed. Says Leech: "Duclos was familiar with the rules, but not enough to really prepare."

Fish have to be weighed on a scale that's been certified by a government agency or the IGFA within the past 12 months. Although it's ideal to have your fish weighed by an official weighmaster, an IGFA official, or a local person familiar with the scale, some anglers who are serious about record fishing travel with their own portable scales. In 1998, the organization had tested 900 portable scales for members. If you're targeting smaller fish, another alternative is to use the scale at a marina or tackle shop. Or do what Leech did when he thought he had a trophy Spanish mackerel: ask for permission to use the scale at your local convenience store. But remember exactly where the store is located, because the IGFA often

The Angle on Catch and Release

WHAT MANY ANGLERS don't realize is that a trophy-sized fish doesn't have to be killed to qualify as a record. These days, many anglers are releasing their prize catches. Although not all situations allow for release, the IGFA encourages it when possible. Among those anglers who have returned their trophy fish to the water are Raz Reid, who released a world-record permit caught on 20-pound (10 kg) tippet that weighed 31 pounds (14.06 kg), and Barry Reynolds, who returned a 33-pound (14.96 kg) northern pike caught on 12-lb (6 kg) tippet back to a Canadian lake. Before you return a fish to its natural environment, be sure you've taken the necessary measurements (see "Weighting Game," page 18). With the proper measurements, you're ready to release. Following are some steps you can take to increase a fish's chance of survival.

1 If you're trolling for big game and using natural bait or scented lures, set the hook quickly when you feel a strike. Most predators can inhale a bait in a second. Setting the hook when you feel a strike can prevent the fish from taking the hook deep in its throat, where it may be difficult or impossible to remove.

2 Once the fish is hooked, try to land it quickly. Studies show that the longer a fish is fought, the less likely it is to survive after release. The only time the fight should be prolonged is when pulling a fish out of deep water. In this case, slow down so the fish can adjust to the changes in pressure and its swim bladder won't expand as dramatically.

3 No matter what material they are made of, hooks don't rust out in a few days. Although it's true that fish are often able to work it loose eventually, it's always best to remove a hook whenever possible. Needle-nose pliers are great for this.

4 The main rule of release is to have the fish in the water with its body just under the surface, and to handle the fish as little as possible. Whether the fish is alongside the boat or in the surf, you want to keep it from thrashing around and injuring itself. If necessary, use a net, but remember that the mesh can remove the mucous coating that protects the fish against infection. Try to use a net made of a soft, nonabrasive material.

5 If you must handle the fish, use a wet glove or towel to touch its body, and avoid sticking your fingers in the eyes or gills. If you bring the fish aboard, lay it on a soft, wetted surface (some charter captains use a towel) and cover its eyes with a wet rag, which some say has a calming effect.

6 Of course, you don't want to bring all species, including sharks, into the boat. If you can't remove the hook easily with a tool while a toothy predator is in the water, cut the leader as close to the mouth as possible.

7 After the hook is removed, revive the fish. The easiest *(continued on next page)*

The Angle on Catch and Release

continued from page 21

method is simply to place the fish in the water, facing into the current or direction of the seas, while you support its belly and hold its tail gently. If the fish needs resuscitation, work it back and forth gently, forcing water through its gills. Don't let go until the fish can swim strongly out of your hands.

requires a scale to be certified after the catch is weighed.

And there are a few other weigh-in requirements.

In the mid-1980s, Donald Angerman from Wayland, Massachusetts, caught an 84-pound (38.10 kg) cod that was a good contender for the 30-pound (15 kg) line class record that had stood since 1967. Angerman was familiar with IGFA regulations and thought he had a legal catch. He even knew the fish had to be weighed on a certified scale. He did so and sent to IGFA, along with his application, the required photos of himself with the fish and the scale. Weeks later, he received word that his catch was disqualified. His photos showed that the fish was weighed on the boat. The bottom line? The IGFA requires this to be done on land, where a truer weight can be determined. Angerman attempted a protest by claiming his boat was docked at the time, but no exception was granted.

"I fish against myself. I don't need a scale to measure my accomplishments."

—Marsha Bierman, 300+ marlin releases

Know Your Fish

Any angler worth his salt may scoff at someone who can't accurately identify a variety of species, but even in the world of record fishing, mistakes can happen.

Captain Rick Gaffney was in Australia on the Great Barrier Reef fly-fishing aboard a reputable game boat when a school of tuna-like fish came up behind the transom. From the bridge, the captain asked Gaffney if he wanted to catch bonito on fly. Gaffney said he would, and then hooked, caught, and brought one to the boat according to the rules. Meanwhile, his fishing companion had his nose in the IGFA book to check the existing record. The fish on the line was a few pounds under the record, so Gaffney released the fish back over the side. Later, he told the captain he thought the fish looked like a kawakawa. The captain said it was. Gaffney was floored. At the time, he didn't know the species is also called bonito in that region. "I think that fish would have been a world record," he says. "But I lost it because communication wasn't complete." Yet like a dedicated record angler, he wouldn't give up. He threw his fly out again, hooked up with another record-sized kawakawa and got it to the boat. But then a shark ate it. Says Gaffney: "That's just one example of how unpredictable and frustrating record fishing can be."

Be Aware

Awareness is a key to record fishing. To increase your chances of success, it helps to be cognizant of any changes in the rules, as well as additions to the book, including new species and line classes. Take special note when it comes to species. Perhaps one of your favorite local fish isn't in the book yet. What many anglers don't realize is that they can get a fish listed in the all-tackle category. All-tackle record claims are considered for all species of fish caught by IGFA rules. To submit a catch, you need to capture that species under the rules, and then the IGFA must deem that it is of substantial weight for its kind. (Typically, they require the fish to be bigger than 50 percent of the species.)

Review the record book and you'll also discover that some of the species listed in the all-tackle section are not included under the line-class categories. The reason? IGFA often relies on public opinion to upgrade a species. Spearfish is an example. This lightweight billfish that is not abundant anywhere was previously listed only on the all-tackle list, but it was upgraded to a full record category after a number of years. Apparently, enough people submitted applications and indicated an interest in catching that species. For that reason, IGFA representatives—there are over 300 around the world—often encourage anglers to submit applications for those offbeat fish not yet in the book.

Do Your Homework

Not all anglers want to target fish that they are very familiar with. For some, stalking unknown species is part of the challenge of record fishing. If you're in search of a species that you have little or no experience with, be aware of the unwritten rule that veteran anglers follow to the letter.

If you're fishing without a captain and crew, you must assume the responsibility for acquiring knowledge about the species, the best places to fish for it, and its availability. The research should be thorough. Gather all the information you can about the species. Read books and magazines. Surf the Web. You can also read the IGFA record book, which includes excellent descriptions of record species, plus illustrations and informative articles on fishing techniques. Check references for spawning times and eating habits. Talk to anyone who is familiar with the species. Then arm yourself with the best equipment and commit the time to pursuing the fish. This is the method that serious record anglers apply to catch their fish. Some, like Steve Zuckerman, take their research one step further.

A secret to angling success, according to this light-tackle pro, is also the ability to think like a fish. Zuckerman is reported to have said that during marathon fights, he started to identify with the fish, gaining an understanding of its character and motivations. Fish really are pretty much like people. Some are tough. Others give up easily.

Breaking the Rules

Before you submit a record to the IGFA, the application process requires the angler and others present for the catch to sign a statement attesting that the fish was caught according to the rules. Back in 1986, one man refused to put his signature on an application. He could not have known that the story surrounding that catch would

Record Strategies: Five Mistakes to Avoid

WHAT ARE THE most common situations that cause a catch to be disqualified as a record by the IGFA? Line that overtests is at the top of the list, but there are other mistakes that are made frequently, according to IGFA president Mike Leech.

1 **The fish doesn't outweigh the existing record.** Too often anglers reference outdated copies of *World Record Game Fishes*. They'll submit applications without realizing that the records they've targeted have already been broken. The best way to avoid making this mistake is to call the IGFA and verify an existing line-class record before you leave the dock (see resources section for telephone number). Some anglers suggest packing a cellular phone in your boat bag, so you can call the organization from the cockpit when the fish on your line looks like it could be a record.

Here's another tip: If your goal is to break an existing line-class record that is less than 25 pounds (11.33 kg), your catch must weigh 2 ounces (0.05669 kg) more than the current mark to qualify as a new record. If the fish you want to beat is over 25 pounds, your catch must exceed its weight by 0.5 percent of the total weight. Therefore, if an existing record weighs 100 pounds (45.35 kg), your catch must tip the scale at 100 pounds, 8 ounces (45.58 kg) to qualify under the IGFA rules.

2 **The scales used to weigh the record fish are not properly certified.** Whether you plan to use your own portable scale (the Chattilon model is popular with many pros), or weigh your catch on the equipment located at a marina or even in a convenience store, remember the IGFA requires that the fish be weighed on a scale that's been certified within the past 12 months.

3 **Anglers don't process their applications in time.** The IGFA requires records submitted from within the United States to reach their office within 60 days of the catch. Applicants outside the U.S. have 90 days.

4 **The catch included terminal gear errors.** Lines, leaders, hooks, and lures must be rigged precisely to IGFA regulations. Yet, sloppy rigging causes many anglers to lose a shot at a record. The most common mistake is rigging the leader or double line too long. Others allow the hooks on a double-hook rig to overlap. Terminal gear requirements for a record are straightforward, and the IGFA strictly enforces these rules.

5 **The application contains contradictory information.** Sometimes the pieces of a complete application just don't match up. For instance, the weight of the fish doesn't match the measurements provided, or the photographs of the catch don't support the given weight and/or measurements. Assemble the required pieces of information carefully, and double-check your work.

become one of the most controversial in IGFA history, a fish that people still talk about today.

On March 16, 1984, Captain Bart Miller had two charter clients aboard his sportfisher, *Black Bart*, which was based in Kona, Hawaii. The anglers, Rankin Smith Jr. and his friend Gary Merriman, had picked a reputable boat to try their hand at big-game fishing. Miller was well known in the sport as one of the world's top captains. Although friends and enemies alike called him egotistical, opinionated, intense, and outspoken, he had earned his lofty position as Hawaii's "Cock of the Dock."

For starters, Captain Miller had proved he could catch fish. By the end of his first season as a charter captain at Kona, he had done the unthinkable: he had caught 87 blue marlin. Miller was considered an innovator of heavy-tackle fishing, too. He was the first to assemble tandem rigs for lures so that they were stiff and the hooks didn't flop around, and he was one of the first to popularize live-bait fishing for marlin in Kona and elsewhere.

Gary Merriman, a tackle-shop owner from Atlanta, hooked a 1,656-pound (751.14 kg) blue marlin that day. It stands as one of the two biggest Pacific marlins ever caught, and as such, it's the kind of fish every angler and captain dreams about. The marlin was boated that day and brought back to the pier, where the application for an all-tackle record was then processed. Later, however, the IGFA would reject the fantastic fish. What happened?

During the fight, Miller called for help to leader the fish. Captain Fran O'Brien came aboard from the boat he was running at the time, *No Problem*. He was on the scene for over two hours, during which time the beautiful creature was landed. Yet during the fight, O'Brien witnessed a variety of infractions against the rules, including use of a leader that was too long. Nevertheless, when the fish was brought back to the dock, Miller processed paperwork to submit the fish for a world record. Captain O'Brien did not sign the documents. Instead, he met with an IGFA trustee the next day and signed a deposition attesting to what he had seen aboard *Black Bart*.

> *"You are what you think you are. . . . I believed I was a great fisherman, and I caught records. If you think it, you are it. That's what it all boils down to."*
>
> —Jerry Dunaway, entrepreneur and multiple record holder

Coming to his own defense, Miller's response to the controversy was that he only went through the motions of processing the claim to appease his charter clients, one of whom wanted to pursue the record. "I was not going to permit the catch to be pushed through as IGFA-legal," he told Jan Fogt of *Marlin* magazine (November 1997).

Can failure to comply with IGFA rules ruin a career? That depends on who you ask. Some say Miller couldn't get a mate job after the marlin incident. Others say the fish brought him notoriety. Today, Miller runs a company in Florida that manufactures fishing lures, and his peers say his reputation and name could be helping him sell more of the artificials.

Nevertheless, Miller's fish will go down in history as one of the most amazing ever

This Pacific blue marlin caught in Hawaii by Gary Merriman aboard the Black Bart is one of the most controversial catches in sportfishing history. This once-in-a-lifetime billfish was disqualified for record status because it was not caught according to IGFA rules. (James Sloan)

caught on rod and reel. And the rejected record? What really happened may always be an unsolved mystery, but it will stand as one of the most famous examples of how not playing by the rules can cause a lot of controversy.

Keep the Faith

We've discussed the general rules for record fishing, and provided you with strategies on how to make the rules work for you. It's important to realize, however, that many of the current world records were probably not achieved by such controlled methods. Just as often, records are the result of happenstance over design. The reality is that anglers who are well prepared and come armed for the record-fishing task with a firm knowledge of the rules will increase their chances of success. If you're out there angling with a focus in mind, the odds have to fall in your favor. Now just keep the faith and remember—records are made to be broken.

3

LIGHT-LINE FEVER AND TALES OF A FANTASTIC FISHING ADVENTURE

Conspicuous consumption" described the mood of the 1980s. A robust economy fattened bank accounts and lifted spirits across the country. Incomes swelled, and the lucky ones were flamboyantly enjoying new levels of personal wealth. The proof was in the boating industry. Manufacturers were moving glossy new fiberglass vessels off their assembly lines faster than you can say "junk bond," and the fevered pitch at marinas nationwide gave one editor at *Forbes* magazine the idea to run a cover story titled "Boat Lust," which discussed the nation's penchant for spending big and living large.

In the sportfishing world, many entrepreneurs were on the cutting edge of this trend. But one angler did things in a bigger way, even in the context of the high-rolling 1980s. Jerry Dunaway combined his love of fishing with innate talents for showmanship, intensity, and making money, and as a result, he rewrote the IGFA record book and changed the way some people would think about fishing for records.

Today, this self-made millionaire from Houston, Texas, is internationally famous as the owner of the *Hooker*, a 48-foot (14.64 m) custom sportfisher with an impressive list of records to its credit. Ironically, however, Jerry's first forays into big-game fishing in the 1970s resembled those of an average tourist. He would charter a good crew and boat at popular fishing destinations such as Hawaii and Mazatlán and hope that he would get a shot at a marlin on heavy tackle. He couldn't have known then that within the next few years fishing for billfish records on light and ultralight line would become his passion and obsession. His new passion would compel him to troll the waters of many oceans; ultimately, he would fine-tune the style that some call "record fishing" today.

At the time, other anglers and captains were focusing their energies on catching big game on line thin enough to sew with,

> *"Many people were afraid to try light line because you have to lose a lot of fish before you get good at it. We're talking about ego here."*
>
> —Captain Skip Smith, Pompano Beach, Florida

Jerry and Deborah Dunaway unwind in the saloon of their sportfishing boat. (Courtesy Jerry Dunaway)

including accomplished anglers such as Leo Cloostermans, George Hogan, Dick Love, and Steve Zuckerman. The media attention to the travels and accomplishments of Dunaway and his crew helped popularize light-line fishing, and today they are credited with making light-line fishing more visible for expert and amateur anglers worldwide. In essence, the *Hooker* crew helped get more people interested in this special type of fishing by proving that it could be done well and fairly.

"When we started, the general public had no clue what four-pound line meant," says Captain Frank "Skip" Smith, who was at the helm of the *Hooker* until 1990. "Many people were afraid to try light line because you have to lose a lot of fish before you get good at it. We're talking about ego here."

Fishing for Dollars

The son of a sheetmetal worker, Jerry grew up in Texas, spent four years in the Air Force, and started a restaurant in Plainview, Texas. Then in 1968, he and his business partner Charles Sims leased a storefront and rented TV sets. By the time Jerry and Sims sold their company in 1983, Remco consisted of 67 wholly-owned stores and 22 franchises across the country renting everything from VCRs to computers. The rental empire gave Jerry the capital to go fishing. In fact, the first thing he bought when his company got successful wasn't a Cadillac, but a boat.

Captain Skip Smith, who ran the Hooker *until 1990, has been called one of the best estimators in sportfishing. He can accurately judge a fish's weight when it's behind the boat. If it looks too small to compete with an existing record, the decision can be made to let the fish go. Being able to estimate weights accurately is just one effective way to target records and protect the resources.* (Courtesy Skip Smith)

This Houston native first made a name in fishing circles while on the tournament scene in the Gulf of Mexico. There, he honed the competitive instincts that later brought him record success. The ultimate tournament was the Poco Bueno out of Port O'Connor. Great billfishing lured anglers to these waters, and big prizes attracted them to this big-purse fishing contest.

To increase his odds of taking the purse one year, nearly $230,000, Jerry had his captain, Skip Smith, charter a plane and fly out over the fishing grounds in search of weedlines the day before. The reconnaissance mission paid off. The boat hooked the fish that was to win it all, a 420-pound (190.50 kg) marlin.

What do you do for a new fishing challenge after winning a quarter of a million dollars? For Jerry, the answer was to invade the waters of Panama. In a three-month period, he caught 42 blue marlin. "Wanting to catch a marlin is one thing," says Jerry. "Maintaining the supporting skills it takes to actually get one to the boat is another thing."

To catch fish consistently, Jerry relied on a crew of dedicated fishermen as intensely focused as he was. The team believed that methodical preparation was essential for success. Smith, a third-generation angler from Fort Lauderdale, Florida, pushed "methodical" to a new level. A record-keeping fanatic, he would constantly take notes on everything from water temperature and color to conditions, tides, and wind speeds. He recorded the location of every fish caught, the bait type and how deep it was running, hook size, and leader size. In all, it was probably a job for a full-time secretary, with so many fish flopping onto the deck.

Yet Jerry's greatest angling achievements were to come aboard the boat he built in the early 1980s: a 48-footer (14.64 m) built by G&S in Destin, Florida, and equipped with a pair of powerful Cummins 903VTA diesel engines at a total cost of about $600,000. It was called the *Hooker*, and in 1984, with Smith at the helm and Trevor Cockle as mate, the 46-year-old angler caught an astounding 86 marlin in a single calendar year. Outdoor writers were comparing his sportfishing success to marlin-hunting legends like Zane Grey and Ernest Hemingway. But unlike those angling stars, Dunaway would cement his reputation with numerous listings in the IGFA record book.

> *"With 4-pound [2 kg] line, you may have to go to free spool, since even water pressure can break this ultralight line."*
>
> —Captain Skip Smith

A Record Obsession Begins

About this time, the IGFA had opened a new 8-pound (4 kg) category for billfish on line test. That intrigued Jerry, who was starting to move away from heavy tackle to light and ultralight lines. In 1986, he planned a trip to Panama with the intention of targeting billfish on that line class.

Fishing out of Tropic Star Lodge in Panama, Captain Smith—lauded as one of the best rod-and-reel swordfish anglers alive—discovered a lot of these fish feeding around a particular piece of bottom. So he made a few trips out to where the fish were and had the crew ready an arsenal of rods and reels equipped with a variety of line classes, including the ultralight monofilament. After nine nights of trolling, the boat had four swordfish records to its credit. Jerry took two of them. The first, a 166-pound (75.29 kg) fish on 12-pound (6 kg) line, toppled a record that had stood since 1968. A few days later, he caught his second record, a 109-pounder (49.44 kg) on 8-pound (4 kg) line test.

Jerry had fished a long time to earn the honor of IGFA record-holder status, but his swordfish records were not the only ones to raise eyebrows. Deborah Maddux was a rookie angler sharing the cockpit with Jerry on that trip. This former legal secretary had less than a year of big-game angling to her credit and zero experience with light tackle. But the Houston native—who later became Jerry's wife—was a good listener and a fast learner. The crew realized that the night they rigged for her an outfit with 16-pound (8 kg) line. Smith knew the women's broadbill swordfish record was open on that line test with a 90-pound (40.82 kg) minimum. When Deborah hooked a fish, the crew was prepared for a long fight in the dark. But Deborah followed their instructions to the letter and got the fish to the surface. The 174-pounder (78.92 kg) put her in the record book. A few nights later, she took a 114-pound (51.70 kg) broadbill on 12-pound (6 kg) test.

Angler Deborah Maddux Dunaway went from being a legal secretary to an expert on handling billfish on ultra-light-line in just a year. Her records, including this 109-pound, 12-ounce (49.80 kg) Pacific sailfish caught on 4-pound (2 kg) line test, are some of the most difficult marks to beat. (Courtesy Jerry Dunaway)

"At the time, I wasn't sure what I had done," says Deborah. "The crew had been talking about records, but I didn't listen to everything they said. I admit I spent some time sunbathing on the transom." For the crew, though, the accomplishments at Panama were unprecedented. "To catch a swordfish on light tackle—that alone is a tough feat," said Captain Skip Smith. "To catch four world records in one week, that is an amazing story, if I do say so myself."

For those anglers who were bent on trying to set or at least equal records for years with no success at all, the accomplishments of the *Hooker* team were a jaw dropper. This crew was still new to the record-fishing game, but they were on the verge of helping Jerry prove one of his personal angling philosophies: the more time an angler spends at the contest, the more likely he is to make stunning catches.

Sportfishing Odyssey

"We want to be the best at everything," said Jerry of his boat and crew in 1987. "I'd like to rewrite all the record books and just have my boat and my crew in all of them. I want to be known as the best angler in the world. It may be ego, but it rings my bells."

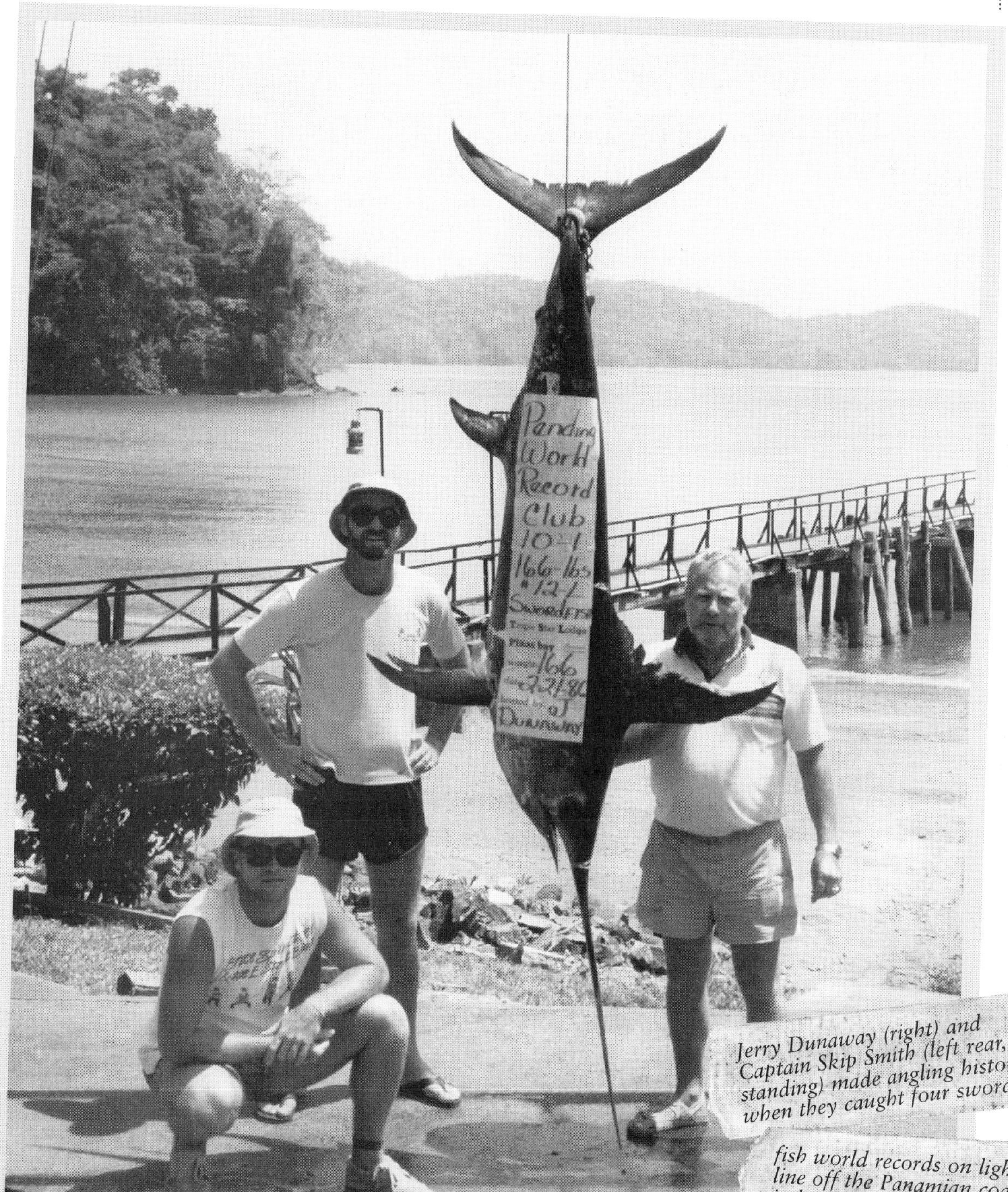

Jerry Dunaway (right) and Captain Skip Smith (left rear, standing) made angling history when they caught four swordfish world records on light line off the Panamian coast in less than one week.
(Courtesy Jerry Dunaway)

See the Light

RECORD-SEEKING ANGLERS with ambitious goals are after big fish on ultralight line. However, fishing for pelagic species offshore on conventional tackle with this type of line requires highly advanced angling skills. To shorten the learning curve, Captain Skip Smith offers the following tips that he learned during his legendary fishing career.

1 **Perfect your presentation.** "Dropping a bait into a fish's mouth is one of the best secrets I have," says Smith, who is credited with developing the switch-bait method for billfish on light line. Most ultralight billfishermen don't just wait for a fish to come up on a trolled line. The reason: It's tough to set the hook that way. "You can't just jerk the rod as you can with heavier tackle," says Smith.

A better strategy is to let the fish hook itself by swallowing the bait. "When you see a billfish approach your bait with his mouth open, drop your rod tip and let the bait drift back to him. If it goes deep, it will pass the bony section of the billfish's mouth, where there's softer tissue for the hook to grab."

Smith notes that this technique resembles one anglers use with heavy tackle, only it's crucial to master on ultralight line. "If the angler can present the bait correctly, hook-up ratio will soar."

Trolling with the switch-bait method is limiting, though, since it works well only on billfish, a species that you can see approach the bait. Trolling light line for other fish, such as tuna, is a different story.

2 **Set the drag properly.** You won't have to break off many fish before you learn the importance of properly setting the drag on light line. "People make the same mistake all the time," says Smith. "One guy puts the rod in a holder on the boat, and another stands on the dock pulling off at a 45-degree angle. That's okay for heavier tackle, where you have more margin for error, but not on this line. Have the angler hold the rod in the normal fighting position and then pull off at a 90-degree angle."

3 **Apply pressure correctly.** With any fish on light line, the first run is critical. When you get the bite, push the drag lever up, come tight, and then get ready to back the drag off. The lighter the line, the farther it has to come off. "With 4-pound [2 kg], you may have to go to free spool," notes Smith, "since even water pressure can break ultralight line." The problem, of course, is that most anglers fear backlash. "That's where experience counts," says Smith. "You have to know where the lightest settings are and where the drag engages." His advice: Play with the gear. It's as simple as working your own baits. Reel them in and let them out day after day and you'll get to know the feel and balance of the tackle. "Working the drag *(continued on next page)*

See the Light

continued from page 34

lever should become as familiar and automatic as starting your car."

4 **Change your backing-down technique for ultralight line.** This tip is for the person running the boat. Upon hookup on heavier tackle, many captains put the boat in reverse and steer for the fish without a concern for belly in the line. However, this technique won't work on ultralight because the line can't withstand the pressure of being dragged through the water. For that reason, the captain has to steer for the place where the line enters the water. Smith recommends using high-visibility line, which is easier for a captain to see and follow.

It was a lofty goal, but Jerry was determined to make it happen. And one of the first things he did to assure his success was buy a mothership, an ocean-going vessel capable of carrying the *Hooker* and crew to the best fishing grounds in the world. Jerry, like many serious record hunters, believed the best way to catch trophy fish on light line was to travel to a hot area during the peak season and get a lot of shots at good-sized fish. Yet he was well-traveled, and he knew that the prime billfishing was often in remote locations, in waters devoid of long-line ships. Traveling to underdeveloped areas can be complex for sport anglers, since boat fuel can be harder to find than civilized accommodations. A mothership would solve the problem by filling the role of fuel dock for the *Hooker* and floating hotel for Dunaway and company.

With a capacity for 39,000 gallons (117 tons), his new mothership—a former oilfield supply vessel that Jerry, with a smirk, dubbed *Madam*—could be self-sustaining for more than a year.

"Wanting to catch a marlin is one thing. . . . Maintaining the supporting skills it takes to actually get one to the boat is another thing."

—Jerry Dunaway, entrepreneur and multiple record holder

Motherships have long been a part of the sportfishing scene. In fact, much of the pioneering exploratory fishing of the 1920s and 1930s was made possible by teaming a big boat with a small boat. Michael and Helen Lerner used the mothership concept in their broadbill expedition off Nova Scotia. Author and angler Zane Grey also used this strategy to explore the world's exotic fishing grounds, including New Zealand and Tahiti, where he caught giant gamefish that were unprecedented at the time. In the 1980s, Grey's spirit was alive and well. A handful of other anglers were trolling the globe in ship combos, too, but

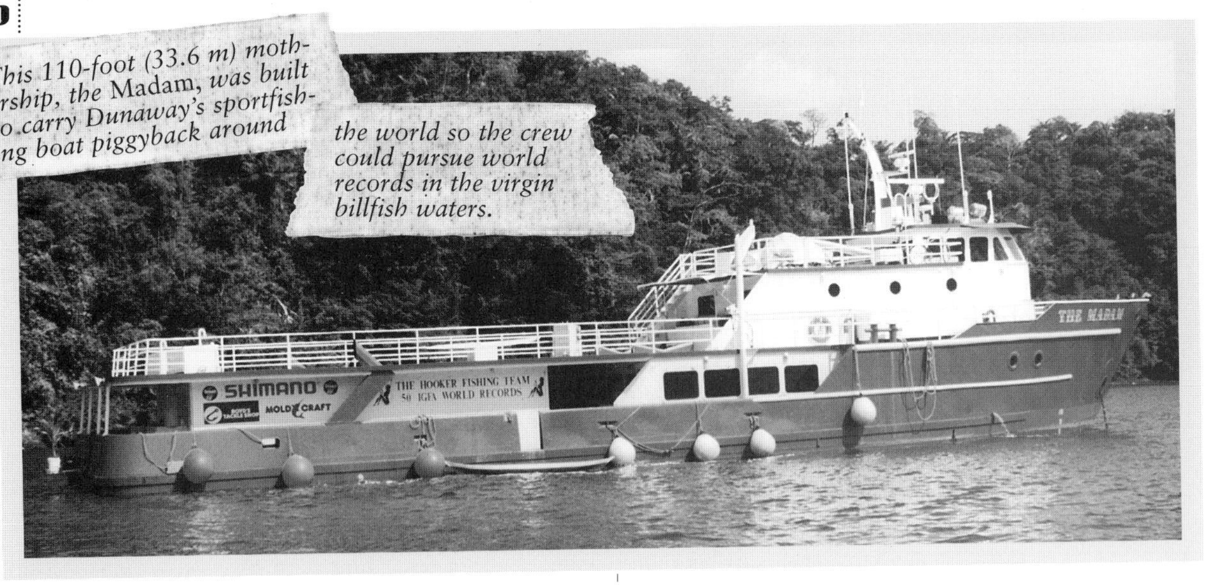

This 110-foot (33.6 m) mothership, the Madam, was built to carry Dunaway's sportfishing boat piggyback around the world so the crew could pursue world records in the virgin billfish waters.

Jerry's operation was unique because it was established with a single mission: record seeking.

Jerry paid $100,000 for the steel-hulled vessel and then spent $400,000 fixing it up. He had the interior gutted, replacing the cargo tanks below with staterooms and extending the deckhouse to accommodate a toney saloon with a state-of-the art entertainment system. In the long run, he invested about $1.2 million in the new boat, which seemed appropriate for a guy who drove a Jaguar with a bumper sticker challenging "Whoever dies with the most toys wins."

Rewriting the record book was a serious goal for Dunaway, and it motivated him to sell his remaining 25 percent share in his business, Remco, so he could fish full time. In 1987, Dunaway, along with Maddux, Smith, and Cockle, began their globe-trolling journey. They left Freeport, Texas, that winter to begin the first leg of their trip, which took them first to Panama, through the canal for fishing along the Pacific coast, and then south to Peru to visit the waters where Alfred Glassel took the all-tackle black marlin. From there, they fished Ecuador, the Caribbean, and Venezuela before crossing the Atlantic to Africa. Later, they fished the Cape Verde Islands before heading home after a 21-month voyage.

> *"If you're good enough to catch fish on a regular basis with conventional lines, the odds of you getting a record on light line are good."*
>
> —Captain Skip Smith

But that was just the beginning. The following winter, the *Madam*, bearing the *Hooker*, left Freeport again, this time in the direction of Costa Rica, where the boats would stop before heading to Hawaii and over to Australia's Great Barrier Reef. It was in all a long, complicated voyage, which on today's shrunken planet is still a great leap for a sportfishing boat.

Keeping the Faith

DUNAWAY AND COMPANY focused their energies on this specialized style of sportfishing after the IGFA created light-line categories. They were record-obsessed, but acquiring a listing in the IGFA book wasn't easy. There was a lot of trial and error in the beginning. "We had more shots at fish than the average guy," says Smith. But even so, "The hardest thing for me was returning to the dock with nothing. That happened for months on end and the mental state was tough."

A bruised ego can turn an angler away from light-tackle fishing faster than a yellowfin tuna can inhale a chunk of bait. Smith's solution for that problem is the same one professional charter crews are using around the world. When trolling a regular spread, fish light tackle on a short position and heavier gear in the long outrigger positions. Even if you miss all shots on the light stuff, you won't get too discouraged if you get one fish on the regular rig.

The short position is a good place to run light line. Since the bait is dragged close to the boat, there's less pressure on the delicate line. (Remember, a ballyhoo on the end of 4-pound [2 kg] test can cause a lot of drag and stress.) In addition, many crews pull teasers short, so this position allows for a lot of shots.

Record-Style Fishing

The *Hooker* was soon lauded as the hottest billfish wagon on the water. Moldcraft, a manufacturer of artificial trolling lures, named a softhead series after the boat, and each member of the crew was sought after by the outdoor writers whose job it was to provide how-to-fish information to the mainstream. But the climb to sportfishing celebrity wasn't always easy, particularly for a crew that was pioneering light-line techniques for big game.

"When the IGFA opened the 8- and 16-pound [4 and 8 kg] line-test categories in the 1980s, there were all those billfish records sitting vacant and crying out for someone to fill them up," says Smith. "Until then I had always thought that fishing light tackle was just an excuse a guy used on the days when everyone else caught fish but him. But Jerry's patience and determination held us together more than anything else. In the beginning, he even showed us some compassion by letting us fish the big outfits about once every ten days. He called it his donation to the crew's mental health, since you can take losing just so many fish on light stuff before going over the deep end."

At that time, there wasn't a lot of information available on fishing light tackle for big fish, aside from the insights published by angler-writer Tred Barta. Nevertheless, Jerry's crew developed their own techniques and modified existing tactics specifically for light-line applications, such as the switch-bait method for billfish. Captain Smith borrowed this concept from Captain Ronnie Hamlin, who had been using it with fly-fishing tackle, and applied it to light line. Here's how it worked:

Light-line record-fishing fever infected other highly skilled anglers, including Stewart Campbell (second from right), shown below with the 714-pound (321.3 kg) blue marlin they caught on 20-pound (10 kg) test. This fish was not a record, but at one time Campbell held the marlin records for the 4-, 8-, 16-, 20-, and 30-pound line test simultaneously. Raleigh Werking, shown at right with a 90-pound (40.82 kg) black drum, is another confirmed light-line record fishing fanatic. (Courtesy Raleigh Werking)

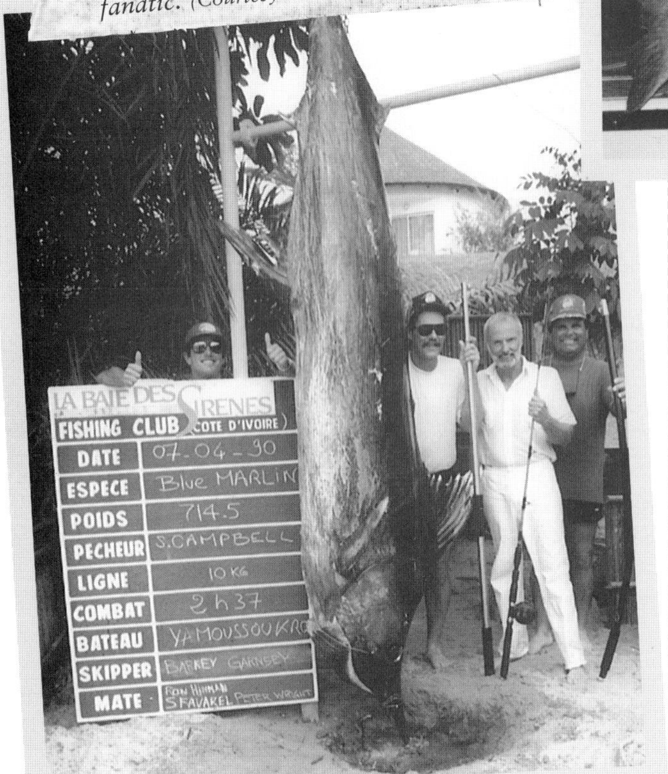

Trolling hookless lures, or teasers, they would tease a fish to the surface. When it broke the surface, they would try to estimate its size and determine which line test to use; the decision was based on the crew's knowledge of existing records. Smith has been called one of the best dead-on guessers in the business, a captain who can accurately judge the weight of a swimming billfish. He would eye the prey and advise the angler in the cockpit on which rod to use (there were always several spooled with a selection of line classes). When the teasers came out of the water, it was the angler's job to substitute a baited hook. This system enabled the crew to tag and release 95 percent of the fish they caught, keeping only those that could be world records. "When I finally haul in a potential record, I feel fabulous," says Jerry. "How else could someone feel when he has just decked the biggest fish that has ever been caught on that line test by anyone in the world?"

The exhilaration was so intense that it dictated Jerry's travel plans for almost ten years. He went where the record fish would be and pursued them with a fierce intensity. Yet ironically, traveling itself was never a goal for him or the crew. "Jerry and Skip would be happy fishing in a swimming pool if they thought there were records there," says Deborah.

Of all the fish that came aboard the

Hooker, Jerry has his favorites. His most memorable was the 231-pound (104.77 kg) blue marlin he took on 8-pound (4 kg) tackle off Africa's Ivory Coast. The record was important to him for two reasons. First, it took him four years to win the record back from Marc Giraud, the Frenchman who broke Dunaway's existing 8-pound (4 kg) record four years before—on Jerry's boat and with Jerry's crew. This catch also taught him something about blue marlin. The fish bit at 11 A.M., but it took Dunaway until midnight to get it into the boat. Yet when mate Trevor Cockle reached out to grab the leader, the big blue made a dive and then came up, piercing its long bill through the layers of fiberglass at the boat's transom. "That woke me up to the fact that I never wore that fish out. Even after 13 hours, the fish just didn't get tired."

Deborah Maddux Dunaway in light-tackle action. (Courtesy Jerry Dunaway)

Jerry, who is also the first male angler to take a blue marlin on 4-pound (2 kg) test, says not all of his fights had happy endings. Dunaway says his most frustrating experience aboard the *Hooker* was in 1989, when fishing 16-pound (8 kg) test in Australia.

He had hooked a black marlin estimated at over 700 pounds (315 kg) and fought it through the day; not once did the fish surface. So he worked the fish through the night, certain that when dawn broke and conditions changed, so would the marlin's stubborn behavior. Finally, after 19 hours, the fish came up.

"And what did he do?" says Dunaway. "Spooled me. Just took off into the sunset." People have said that a poor day of fishing will darken Dunaway's ebullient Texas charm, and this occasion was no different. "I moped the whole next day. Drank a lot of whiskey. What else am I gonna do? I fought a fish all that time just to have him come up and make a fool out of me."

One of the most impressive credentials for the *Hooker* is the fact that many of the boat's records are rare 20-to-1 catches, where the weight of the fish exceeds the breaking strength of the line by more than 20 times; some are better than 30-to-1. Deborah, in particular, was the angler making many of these outstanding catches. Some were frustrating for the woman who was only 5 foot, 1 inch tall and 103 pounds (155 cm, 46.4 kg), including the 380-pound (172.36 kg) black marlin she caught in Panama on 16-pound (8 kg) test in 1994 after eight years of trying for the record.

For a small angler, 16-pound test can be heavy and unmanageable tackle. That's one reason Deborah calls her fight with the marlin "the most exhausting and nerve-wracking thing I have ever done in my life." She hooked the fish at 8:45 A.M. and fought it for the next nine hours and 45 minutes.

"I got so tired I believed I couldn't go on, but Jerry and the crew encouraged me," Deborah told *International Angler* (March/April 1994). "During this time, we lost our generator, which meant no spreader lights. Jerry told me I'd have to add more drag and try to get the fish before dark. By this time I was ready to do anything just to end the ordeal." So she pushed up the drag and got the fish to the boat, where it broke the leader. Fortunately, the crew was swift with a gaff, allowing Deborah to cinch the record.

The Next Frontier

After a decade of fishing for records at a fevered pace, the man who believes in constantly setting goals is formulating new ones. In 1999, the *Madam* and the *Hooker*, which is now captained by Trevor Cockle, will be sold to a new owner, and Dunaway has a new sportfishing boat on order at G&S. He'll take it to Madeira, where he plans to live half the year and fish, not for records, but for big, 1,000-pound (453.59 kg) billfish on heavy tackle. Granders are his next goal, and you can bet he'll pursue them with the same intensity that fueled his passion for records. As for Deborah, she'll be right there in the cockpit; she plans to stay with light tackle and search for more records.

> *"Dropping a bait into a fish's mouth is one of the best secrets I have."*
>
> —Captain Skip Smith

As for the records taken by Dunaway and company over the years, many have been toppled—one of Dunaway's friendly adversaries, Stewart Campbell, took the blue marlin records on 4-, 8-, 16-, 20-, and 30-pound line test and made history by holding them simultaneously. Yet fallen records are proof that more people are discovering the allure of light-line fishing.

For those who want to employ Dunaway's style of targeting records, there are opportunities to break other existing marks on light line. Some are daunting, but with determination they could fall. The women's marks on marlin, for instance, are obtainable, says Smith. Yet big game is only one challenge. Today, many anglers are employing light-

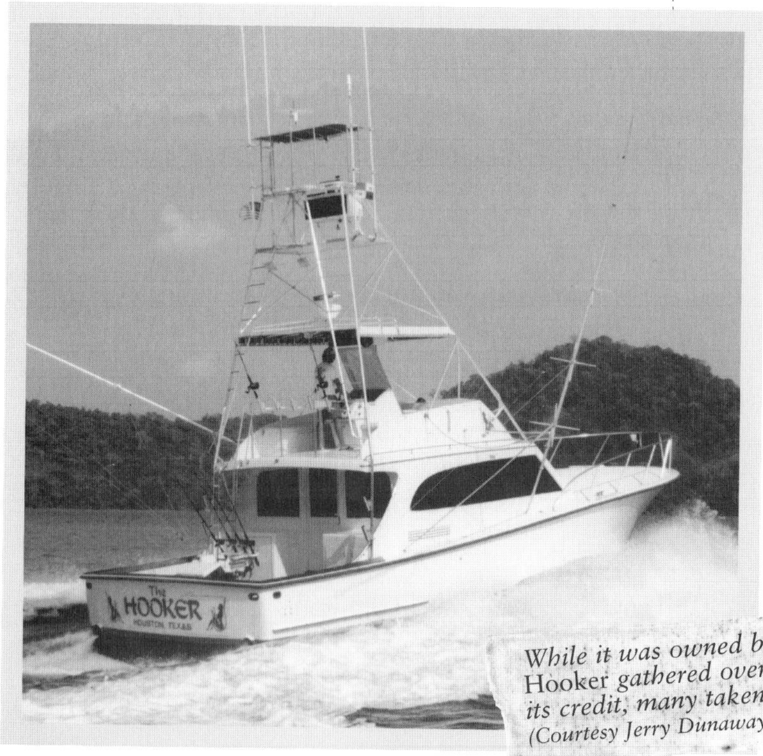

While it was owned by Dunaway, the Hooker gathered over 80 records to its credit, many taken with light line. (Courtesy Jerry Dunaway)

Tackle Tips

A GOOD CREW, a good boat, and skill are essential for the ultralight angler. After skill, tackle is the most important component. A reel with a smooth drag and a rod that will absorb the stress when the fish runs or jumps are critical to success.

Most light- and ultralight-tackle specialists prefer conventional tackle because of the control it provides. Above 20-pound (10 kg) line, a good-quality production rod will serve your needs, but below 20-pound experts like Jerry Dunaway believe you need a custom rod with extra line guides and certain performance features.

Standard rods come with 6 to 8 guides; custom ultralight rods will have anywhere from 12 to 16 guides. The extra guides help reduce friction. "A lot of fishermen seem to think the fish causes the line to break, but 90 percent of the time it's the guides that fray the line," says Captain Skip Smith. Properly placed rod guides provide even pressure on the delicate line, preventing it from touching the rod and breaking.

During his years aboard the *Madam* and the *Hooker*, Dunaway and company worked with Boyd's Custom Tackle of Fort Lauderdale, Florida, to develop the desired action for 2-, 4-, and 8-pound rods. "Many light-tackle anglers prefer a slow-action rod similar to a fly rod for 8-pound [4 kg] line and below," says Dunaway. "In the beginning, each of my ultralight rods was a little different. The rod for 2-pound [1 kg] line had a flexible tip and a lot of give to about halfway down the blank. The rod for 4-pound [2 kg] line had a lot of flex in the top 12 inches [30 cm]. The 8-pound rod is graphite composite and therefore much stiffer." However, even with all their experience, Dunaway was constantly tinkering with the tackle.

As for maintenance, one of the most important things the crew of the *Hooker* did was to change the drag washers and line frequently—they did so after each fish they caught. They also kept reels lubricated. Captain Skip Smith would prep reels with a special grease, which he says was particularly effective with 2- and 4-pound (1 and 2 kg) line. Lubricating the reels allows the line to come right off the reel, without the initial inertia that sometimes occurs when a fish first takes the bait.

So which line test should a newcomer to light tackle try first? Dunaway's advice would be to start with 16- or 8-pound (8 or 4 kg) tackle; which size depends on how big a fish you're trying for. For the most part, what you need to do is spend time getting to know how much pressure the string will take before moving on to the next lighter line class. Dunaway says people were amazed when he set his first records on 2- and 4-pound (1 and 2 kg) line, "but what most of them didn't realize is that it took me a year and a half before I was ready to move down from 8-pound [4 kg]."

line techniques on less glamorous fish—fluke, flounder, and rockfish, for instance. "If you're good enough to catch fish on a regular basis with conventional lines, the odds of you getting a record on light line are good," says Smith.

If you ask Deborah why she thinks her husband is a trailblazer, she won't only ref-

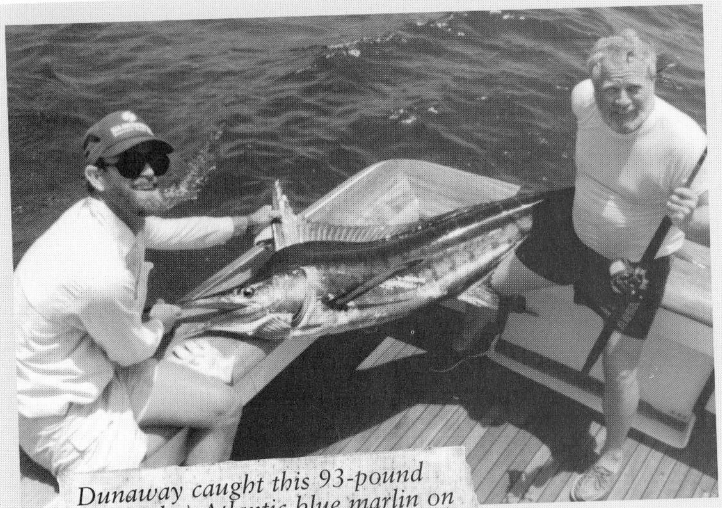

Dunaway caught this 93-pound (42.18 kg) Atlantic blue marlin on 4-pound (2 kg) line test in 1988 in the Cape Verde Islands, establishing a record. Talk about frustration! Dunaway claims he lost 52 blue marlin on 4-pound test before capturing this fish. (Courtesy Jerry Dunaay)

erence his records. She also emphasizes that his contribution to fishing has been his eagerness to share information with others, making it possible for them to experience the thrill of fishing remote locations and to understand the intricacies of light-line techniques and record fishing.

As for Dunaway, he never doubted that he would be a successful angler. "I was as dedicated to fishing as I was to my business. That success is based on the philosophy I live by. Essentially, I believe that you are what you think you are. I believed I was a millionaire and I became one. I believed I was a great fisherman, and I caught records. If you think it, you are it. That's what it all boils down to."

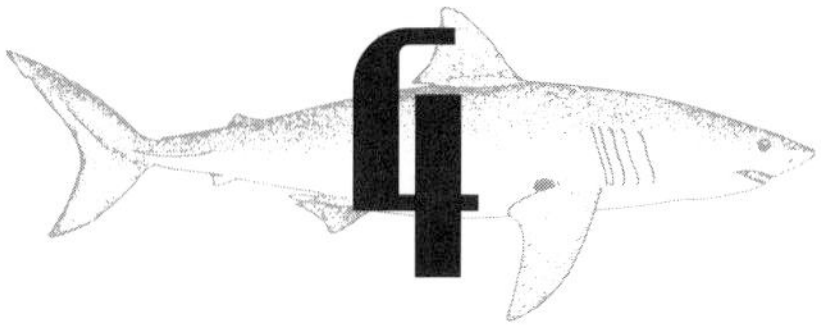

4

WOMEN AND RECORDS

I'm always floored when I meet a person who's surprised to discover that women are skilled anglers. The last time I encountered someone who chose to spread the rumor that females and fish don't mix was about 15 years ago, but that guy also referred to his wife as "the little woman" and regularly told his male fishing buddies that a female on board will jinx any fishing trip.

It seems the myth that females don't fish still exists, despite the fact that women account for approximately one-third of all anglers casting lines today.

Where that rumor got started is anybody's guess, but it's probably been perpetuated by an outdated image of a "fisherman." For those not close to the sport, the word sometimes conjures a picture of a man buckled into a fighting chair at the back of a bobbing boat in a gray and rolling sea, a bearded Hemingway lookalike who stoically struggles against a humongous fish. Anglers, particularly the world-record kind, aren't generally assumed to be women because some people haven't awakened to the fact that females possess the strength, stamina, and finesse to pull in trophy-sized fish. The proof that women do, however, is in the IGFA record book.

Women have been contributing phenomenal record catches since the book's first publication. In recent years, a group of highly dedicated women have been acquiring new records on a regular basis, even in the highly coveted billfish categories. Who are these women? One insider says that angling women with the most records are often those who are married to men who take them fishing. That seemed to be a gross generalization at first, but after reviewing the record book, I realized there was a grain of truth to what he said. So I asked Jeanne

"You have to know the rules, decide which fish you're going after, then choose your gear and just try it. It's a learning process. But if you're serious about records, you'll keep trying. The main thing is don't get discouraged. So many people do."

—Deborah Maddux Dunaway,
first person to hold records
on all nine billfish species

Jeanne DuVal, shown here with a 52-pound (23.58 kg) wahoo caught on 8-pound (4 kg) test, believes light tackle is a good choice for many women. "I don't have the brute strength required to work with heavy tackle, but I do have stamina, which is necessary to catch trophy fish on light tackle."

DuVal why fewer women pursue records on their own without pairing up with men. This angling veteran with over 50 records to her credit gave me some good food for thought.

When DuVal started fishing with her husband William in the mid-1960s, it was typical for many women her age to quit their jobs and forfeit a salary after they were married to raise children. But it takes money to pursue any worthwhile hobby, and fishing is no exception, particularly when it comes to records. That was one reason women of DuVal's generation went fishing with their husbands: the men were paying the fees to fish. Certainly, many women—then and now—like the idea of sharing a sport with their spouse. But today, things are changing, says DuVal. More women are discovering the sport on their own, and they're committed to fishing, since they have the financial wherewithal to do so.

That's surely one reason more women are pursuing records today. The IGFA recently opened new record opportunities for women as a result of increased interest and participation. For instance, in January 1998, the IGFA created two separate categories in the fly rod class, one for men and one for women. Prior to January 1998, there was a single category for both sexes in the saltwater and freshwater categories. The decision—prompted in part by a petition drawn up by Jodie Pate, the wife of fly-fishing legend Billy Pate—opened hundreds of records for women. This change, coupled with the addition of some new species and expanded line-class categories, means that the time is right for women who want to pursue record fish.

One of the Pioneers

The sportfishing world was not always so open to women. In fact, there was even a time when their successes were trivialized or, worse, suspect. Mrs. Keith Spalding trolled lines back in those days (as we can tell by the omission of her first name from the records). The wife of a member of the Tuna Club of Santa Catalina Island, Spalding toughed it out on rough seas, and in 1921 her efforts boated her a 426-pound (193.22 kg) broadbill swordfish, the most coveted big-game fish of that time. And according to George Reiger, author of *Profiles in Saltwater Angling,* not only was the catch spectacular, it also infuriated Tuna Club member Zane Grey. It seems Spalding bruised the trophy-sized ego of this best-selling western writer and celebrated angler when he learned her fish beat the one he caught the year before by 8 pounds (3.62 kg). Grey, who had dubbed the broadbill "the greatest gladiator of them all," blew his cool and accused Spalding of recruiting help to catch the big fish.

Women fishing in salt water started to put a dent in the record books in the 1930s and 1940s. Those years were known as the Golden Age of big-game angling, when the oceans were flush with billfish and giant tuna and the sport was coming into its own. In *Reel Women: The World of Women Who Fish*, author Lyla Fogia writes, "Women of this era defied the prevailing mystique of the sport; that it took brute strength, more than endurance and finesse, to land fish many times an angler's own weight—especially since most of these women barely tipped the scales at 100 pounds (45 kg) themselves and were handling Paul Bunyan–sized tackle."

In the 1950s a new breed of dedicated anglers was stepping up to the transom, including Eugenie Marron, who captured four records in 1954. Eugenie's 772-pound (350.17 kg) swordfish on 80-pound (37 kg) test is considered one of the phenomenal catches of that decade.

The fishing bug first bit Eugenie after her marriage to Lou Marron, a dedicated angler whose 1,182-pound (536.15 kg) sword-

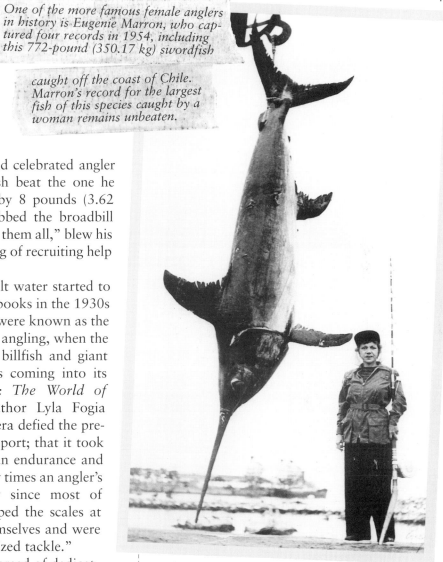

One of the more famous female anglers in history is Eugenie Marron, who captured four records in 1954, including this 772-pound (350.17 kg) swordfish caught off the coast of Chile. Marron's record for the largest fish of this species caught by a woman remains unbeaten.

"From that time forward I was always fated to be more at home in jeans on a wildly tossing boat than at the finest party in the smoothest silks."

—Eugenie Marron, mentor for female anglers in the 1950s

"Bill never told me he loved me until he found out I didn't get seasick and could fish. . . . As I fell in love with him, I fell in love with the sport. But I don't fish for records because of him. You have to love the sport to pursue records. That's the number one thing."

—Jeanne DuVal, 50+ records

fish taken off the coast of Chile in 1953 was the largest gamefish ever taken on rod and reel at that time. Ironically, Eugenie's transformation from "normal girl to dedicated angler" occurred in the middle of a party in New Jersey.

She was sitting on a piano in a black velvet dress when a local skipper came to announce there were tuna off to the northeast. Excited, her husband asked her to prepare to go. "If you think I'm going fishing at 12 o'clock on a Saturday night," she replied, "you can start thinking all over again." Yet when Lou said good-bye, Eugenie followed him. Once on the boat, she changed into a pair of dungarees. "And with that change of costume my whole life turned around," she wrote in her book *Albacora: The Search for Giant Broadbill.* "From that time forward I was always fated to be more at home in jeans on a wildly tossing boat than at the finest party in the smoothest silks."

That night she landed a 430-pounder (195.04 kg) that was the first giant tuna taken by a woman off the coast of the United States.

A Woman of the 1990s

Since the 1950s, many more women have made fishing history.

Jocelyn Everett is well known internationally as crew aboard *Northern Lights*, a 37-foot (11.3 m) Merrit sportfishing boat based in Kona, Hawaii. Jocelyn owns and runs the boat with her husband Captain Kelly Everett. Anglers worldwide with a penchant for big fish on light and ultralight line consult the Everetts for advice on how to catch record fish, and the Everetts have good answers. Their boat has numerous records to its credit; at least five belong to Jocelyn, who says her first trophy fish was no accident.

The Everetts grew up near each other in Alaska, where they fished together for salmon, halibut, and the like. They married in 1980 and moved to Kona after Kelly was badly injured in an accident while working on the Alaska Pipeline. Because it was difficult for Kelly, who wears a prosthesis, to handle conventional heavy tackle, the Everetts started fishing lighter line when they landed in the waters of this billfish mecca in the Pacific. And they got plenty of practice: in one two-year period they fished a total of 600 days. During that time, they educated themselves about the IGFA and evaluated their chances for record status. In 1985, they bought a 1963 Merrit, refurbished the classic sportfishing boat, and put it into charter. That's when they went record fishing seriously.

"We would look in the book and we would target a line class to fish," she says. The result? Her husband eventually captured one of history's most fantastic records: a 1,103-pound (500.54 kg) Pacific blue on 30-pound (15 kg) line. As for Jocelyn, four of her records still stand. They include a

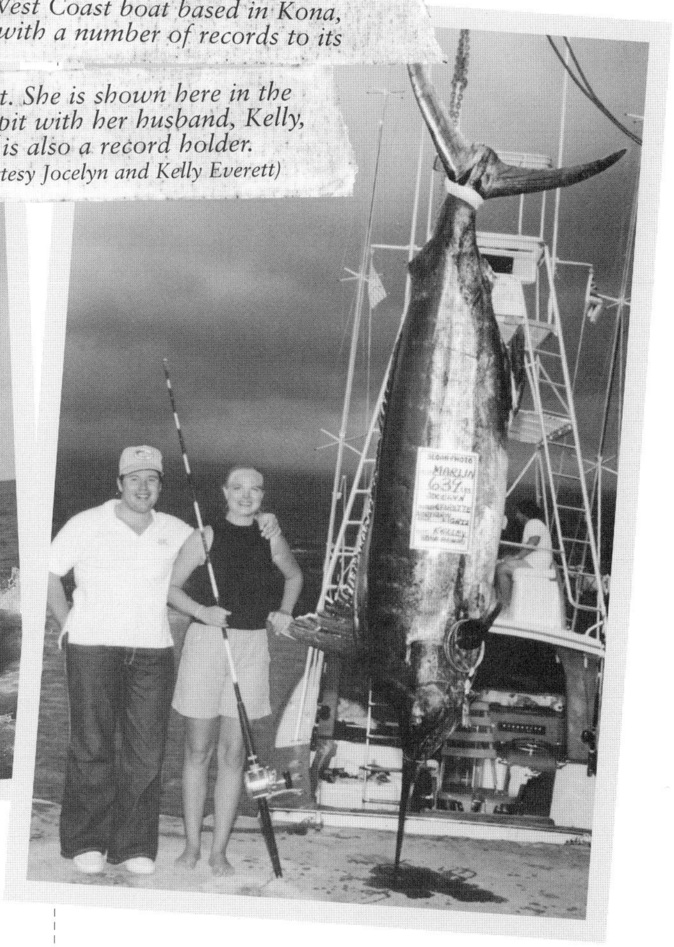

Jocelyn Everett is both record holder and former crew aboard Northern Lights, a well-known West Coast boat based in Kona, Hawaii, with a number of records to its credit. She is shown here in the cockpit with her husband, Kelly, who is also a record holder.
(Courtesy Jocelyn and Kelly Everett)

639-pound (289.84 kg) Pacific blue marlin on 30-pound (15 kg), a 302-pound (136.90 kg) thresher shark on 30, and a 120-pound (54 kg) yellowfin tuna on 16 (8 kg).

Her first record, the tuna, is among the fish she is most proud of, and she uses the yellowfin to illustrate her belief that women have specific angling advantages over men.

"Fighting that tuna was as physically exhausting as giving birth," says this mother of three. She had left the dock that day in search of a record, and when she hooked the yellowfin, she knew she had a fish that could get her into the IGFA book. So she fought it for 10 hours, even after repeatedly bringing it to the surface and then watching the fish steam back to the deep, taking all of her line with it. "I went a long time on that one, but I've fished with men who couldn't. They had the strength to get a fish like that, but not the stamina. When men fight big game, they're more apt to put the drag on and muscle the fish in. But you can't do that on light line. Women don't rely on their strength; they have the patience to slowly work the fish back up. That's the skill I used to beat the tuna on 16 [8 kg]. It's one of the toughest fish in the world. It won't jump like a marlin and give you a chance to rest. It just goes straight down and you can't stop it. It can bring football players to their knees."

There were times during that fight when fatigue would make Jocelyn feel "zoned out." That happens to a lot of anglers battling trophy fish for long periods, she says. And when you're really tired, it's easy to break off a fish by making a stupid mistake.

One of the ways she avoids losing fish to exhaustion is with support from the crew. "They give me simple instructions, like when to drop my drag, and they talk to me all the time. That's important. When you're on a fish for a while, there can be a few seconds when you forget the simplest technique, but it only takes a few seconds for a fish to break the line."

"When men fight big game, they're more apt to put the drag on and muscle the fish in. But you can't do that on light line. Women don't rely on their strength; they have the patience to slowly work the fish back up."

—Jocelyn Everett, 5+ records

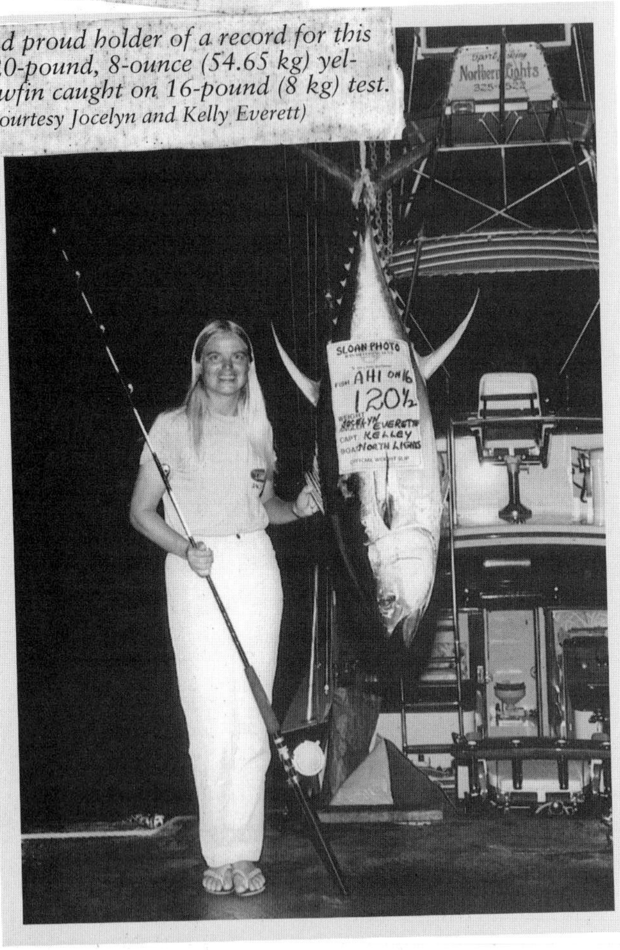

"Fighting that tuna was as physically exhausting as giving birth," says Jocelyn Everett, mother of three and proud holder of a record for this 120-pound, 8-ounce (54.65 kg) yellowfin caught on 16-pound (8 kg) test. *(Courtesy Jocelyn and Kelly Everett)*

That's one reason the Everetts run their boat with not one but two crew in the cockpit at all times, one to leader and the other to gaff. On some other charter boats, the captain will do double duty at the wheel and in the cockpit assisting a single crew member. But the Everetts think that strategy could lower an angler's odds of catching a record fish. They also suggest that anglers book a minimum of three days aboard a charter boat. "It generally takes that long to get the team together on procedures," says Jocelyn.

Today, Jocelyn spends much of her time at home raising three children but plans to return to *Northern Lights* full-time in a few years. In the meantime, she's formulating future record-setting goals. She tells other women in search of new angling challenges that the key to record-fishing success for big game is the right boat with the appropriate tackle and trained crew. On *Northern*

Another female angling luminary is Chisie Farrington, who chronicled the fishing exploits of her female friends in Women Can Fish. *She also earned the respect of her angling peers for catching five broadbill swordfish in a decade. Here she stands with the 674-pound (305.71 kg) bluefin she caught off Watch Hill, Rhode Island, in 1950.*

Pam Basco is one of the female anglers making great strides in record fishing today. She is shown here with a 203-pound, 8-ounce (92.30 kg) yellowfin tuna caught on 20-pound (10 kg) line class. Her advice to record seekers: fish with a crew that's as excited about the challenge as you are.

Lights, all the gear is IGFA rated, and the Everetts take pains to instruct anglers on rules, including pulling your own rod. The Everetts turn time in the cockpit into a learning experience for the anglers, and in the process they make record fishing fun.

"I like their style," says record holder Pamela Basco, an IGFA trustee and a Texan who regularly travels to Hawaii to fish light line with the Everetts. "They get as excited about it as I do. That's important when you're shooting for a record. The crew has to share your goals. It's also important that they know what to expect of you. You don't want a complete learning experience every time you get on a boat. When you know how things are going to be, you can increase your odds of getting a fish. For instance, for the past 12 years I've fished at least once a year with the Everetts. As a result, I have caught five world records from their boat."

See the Light

In the last decade, women have been making headlines with record fish on light line. Among the names most frequently heard in charter boat circles are Marg Love, Terri Kittredge Andrews, and Liz Hogan—Hogan alone holds four of the most difficult records in the tarpon category, from 2-pound (1 kg) line up to 8-pound (4 kg). She caught the 4-pound (2 kg) record during a charter in Marathon, Florida, in 1996. The 134-pound, 3-ounce (60.87 kg) monster was 43 times heavier than the breaking strength of her line. On that same trip, Hogan landed a 141-pound, 9-ounce tarpon (64.21 kg) on 8-pound (4 kg) line and then let it go while it was still alive. That fish was a 28-to-1 catch and the first tarpon world record ever released.

The popularity of light line has grown tremendously since the 1980s, and for that reason, many experts say it's getting tougher for an amateur to get a record on this type of tackle. Yet many of sportfishing's most skilled women say that light line and even fly line are better suited for females. One reason is light tackle is easier to handle. For some women, it can be tougher to fight the heavy tackle than to fight a fish.

All of Jeanne DuVal's 50-plus records have been taken on light or fly line. "Heavy tackle can turn a fight into a long, grueling one for anyone, but particularly for women," she says. "I don't have the brute strength required for that type of fishing, but I do have stamina, which is necessary to catch trophy fish on light tackle." Some anglers also contend that light tackle makes sense financially for anglers who don't have thousands of dollars to devote to fishing.

It's not uncommon for well-traveled anglers to start fishing heavy tackle for big fish and then discover light line after the thrill of catching the heaviest fish wears off and a new challenge is required. But like a number of her female peers, DuVal skipped the heavy gear and started fishing line 20 pounds (10 kg) and under from the start. "I never had that big fish urge. I love to see a leaping marlin, but I want to catch it on light line."

Jeanne, who grew up in North Carolina, never really fished until she met her future husband in 1960. A Virginia native, Bill was a talented angler who was fishing light tackle in the 1960s with sportfishing legends like Joe Brooks. "Bill never told me he loved me until he found out I didn't get seasick and could fish. He took me to Key West, put me on an amberjack on 30-pound [15 kg] line and taught me to fish. As I fell in love with him, I fell in love with the sport. But I don't fish for records because of him. You have to love the sport to pursue records. That's the number one thing."

Today, the couple still shares their passion for fishing. Between the two of them, they hold 80 records. Some have been caught on their own boat near their summer home on the Outer Banks of North Carolina. But the DuVals

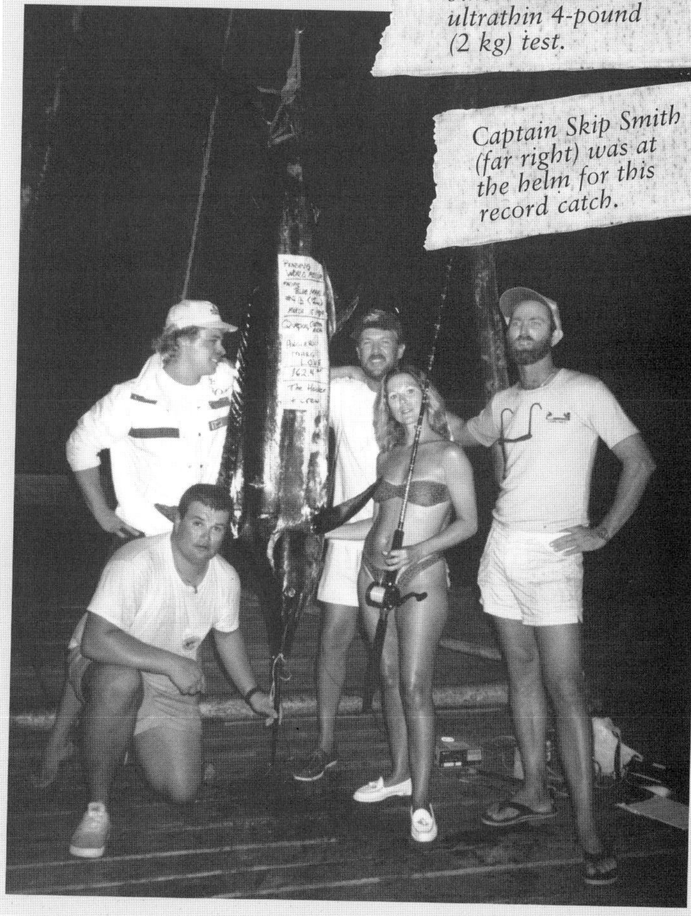

Another well-known big-game angler is Marg Love, who caught this 162-pound, 6-ounce (73.65 kg) Pacific blue marlin on ultrathin 4-pound (2 kg) test.

Captain Skip Smith (far right) was at the helm for this record catch.

> *"The crew has to share your goals. It's also important that they know what to expect of you. You don't want a complete learning experience every time you get on a boat. When you know how things are going to be, you can increase your odds of getting a fish."*
>
> —Pam Basco, 12+ records

enjoy fishing with and learning new skills from talented captains, so they travel when they can make time away from the real estate development business they operate in Richmond, Virginia.

Jeanne was on a charter boat fishing about 80 miles west of Key West in the Dry Tortugas with Captain R. T. Trosset when she caught what she defines as her most impressive fish, a 52-pound (23.58 kg) wahoo on 8-pound (4 kg) line in March 1993. It was sunset, and Trosset was throwing the last of his live baits into the water. Jeanne was in the cabin putting on a rain suit in preparation for the ride back in when the captain started yelling about a wahoo. "I grabbed the rod and put it over. Forty-five minutes later, R.T. says 'You got him.' That's when I remembered that I had twisted the wire. When I told Bill and R.T., their faces went white." With low confidence in Jeanne's rigging skills, the men mentally conceded to defeat. But within a half hour, she had the fish.

Jeanne's husband, who thinks the wahoo was one of her finest records, also believes that "women make better light-tackle anglers than men." Why? One theory: "they don't have as much muscle in their arms, so there's less tendency for their arms to cramp up during a fight that lasts a few hours." That's the physical difference. Emotionally, says Bill, women have a better temperament. "They have more patience and they don't get as upset at losing record fish as men do."

"If you get angry, you can't have fun," says Jeanne.

Today, she is fishing fly line frequently. She's challenged by the new records open for women, even though she's one of few females to have acquired a fly record (black sea bass on 8-pound [4 kg] tippet) before the category was split. "To catch a record, you have to know what's possible," she says. "It's not difficult to catch a record, but it can be tough to make yourself aware of what's open."

To Boldly Go Where No Man Has Gone Before

Every good angler has a mentor, and for many record-hunting women today, that mentor is Deborah Maddux Dunaway. Although her globe-trotting lifestyle and penchant for big fish on light line (see chapter 3) is worlds away from the type of fishing the average woman does, Deborah set a standard for many female anglers when she achieved something no one had done: in 1993 she became the first person ever to catch an IGFA record on all nine species of billfish. Even more impressive, all nine records were standing simultaneously. The feat was so phenomenal that it was lauded in newspapers and magazines across the country, including those that don't normally cover fishing. Even the *National Enquirer* wrote her up as "the world's best fisherman."

Shown here with one of the many billfish she's captured in her angling career, Deborah Maddux Dunaway is a mentor for many women seeking records today. (Courtesy Jerry Dunaway)

Ironically, she made history with the capture of a small, scrappy 26-pound, 8-ounce (12.02 kg) short-billed spearfish.

Prior to the catch, which was boated in Hawaii aboard the *Humdinger* with Captain Jeff Fay, the spearfish was the only one of nine billfish species she had no record on. Because of its scarcity, the spearfish is considered by some to be the most difficult of all billfish to target and capture. Even in Kona, where most of the record spearfish have been taken, they're never as plentiful as the larger blue marlin. Most years, spearfish—the smallest of all the billfish—will show up sometime during the spring or summer months in numbers that make catching them a distinct possibility, but the date of their arrival is impossible to predict.

When Fay called Deborah and her husband Jerry Dunaway in Texas with the news that the spearfish were off Kona, they canceled a previously planned trip to Costa Rica and hopped a flight to Hawaii.

Deborah still remembers that day and how the fish sounded after she set the hook. Over 20 yards (18 m) of the fine fishing line slipped down into the 1,000-fathom water. Only an expert can manipulate the drag setting to avoid breaking the line under these conditions, but Deborah's cool reactions, even in the excitement of the moment, attested to her years of angling experience.

The fight dragged on for three hours before the crew decided to increase the drag, although ever so slightly. Fay maneuvered the boat to avoid putting a belly in the line, which can create friction and break the delicate thread. That's when the swivel popped above the surface. The fish was brought in and, as everyone aboard yelled and cheered, Deborah burst into tears.

Deborah's success was motivational for many anglers, including Pam Basco. "She was a trailblazer. She got me interested in pursuing records." In addition to raising eyebrows with her advanced light-line techniques, Deborah taught some people how to target record fish, including Basco, who says, "You have to know the rules, decide which fish you're going after, then choose your gear and just try it. It's a learning process. But if you're serious about records, you'll keep trying. The main thing is don't get discouraged. So many people do."

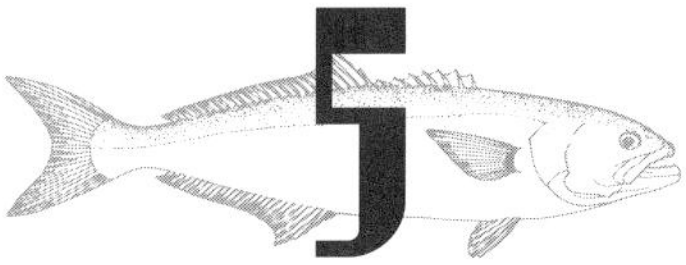

5

FLY FISHING FOR WORLD RECORDS IN SALT WATER

In recent years, saltwater fly-fishing has been catching on worldwide with astonishing popularity, from Florida to Maine, along the Gulf of Mexico, on the West Coast, and throughout the world. Both freshwater and saltwater fly anglers who were raised on conventional gear are discovering the drama and excitement of taking big saltwater fish on this light tackle. It's one of angling's fastest-growing sports, and that's reflected in the IGFA record book.

Having watched the phenomenal growth of this unique fishing form, the IGFA expanded the fly-fishing category to give more anglers the opportunity to shoot for records. For instance, as more anglers were drawn to the unique and fascinating challenge of hooking and fighting big ocean species such as sailfish and marlin on this tackle, the IGFA anticipated the need for a stronger tippet class than the existing 2-, 4-, 6-, 8-, 12-, and 16-pound categories. In 1991, a new 20-pound-class (10 kg) tippet category was introduced. (The IGFA defines the tippet as the smallest or lightest portion of the leader.)

Another major expansion occurred in 1998, when a separate category for women was instituted in saltwater fly-fishing. Although saltwater records for conventional tackle are separated into categories for men and women, the decision to do the same for fly-fishing caused some controversy in the angling community, particularly among women who wanted to compete on the same playing field as men. However, the IGFA maintained that a single category represented a disadvantage for women, particularly in the heavier tippet classes, such as 20, where gear can require more strength to handle.

"Discover the drama of taking big saltwater fish on fly."

The Allure of Salt Water

What factors are drawing more anglers to fly rods and salt water? Although this type of gear has been restricted to small freshwater gamefish like trout, salmon, and bass for centuries, veteran fly anglers have been discovering that salt water breeds stronger fish that are more challenging to hook and fight, and it nurtures faster species that make their freshwater counterparts look like amateur

In recent years, anglers have discovered the thrill of targeting records on saltwater fly. Here, author-angler Jack Samson is shown with his record roosterfish, which he caught in Costa Rica on August 20, 1988. Taken on 16-pound (8 kg) tippet, the fish weighed 31 pounds, 12 ounces (14.37 kg). (Courtesy Jack Samson)

swimmers. Author-angler Lefty Kreh summed it up in *Fly Fishing in Salt Water*: "No stocked fish roam the seas. These are fish straight from God's hand and they are in prime condition. The brown trout may frustrate you, but a permit will drive you mad. It's an extremely strong fish, perhaps one of the strongest in the sea. I kissed the first one I caught. It weighed only five pounds."

"Fish for pleasure first and let the record thing be secondary. . . . I've seen people become obsessed with that goal, and have it kill their interest in the actual fishing. Fish for fun first, but to increase your odds of obtaining a record, set up according to IGFA rules."

—Del Brown, permit angler extraordinaire

Although some anglers have been targeting records on saltwater fly gear for decades, there's been an increase in the number of applications the IGFA receives annually only in recent years. The increased competition has done good things for the sport. It's motivated experts to develop new tackle and techniques that benefit all anglers. In addition, it's inspired pioneering people to travel to places that haven't been fished with fly, to explore the potential both inshore and offshore, and to document the size of fish living in these areas. As a result, anglers are equipped with information on where the best opportunities are for a variety of species.

For instance, more fly anglers have been discovering the prolific fisheries in the Pacific, including Christmas Island, where some say a hard-working angler can average better than 30 bonefish a day on fly. Fantastic numbers of giant trevally have been discovered, too; in fact, five of the seven tippet-class records were taken here since 1994. Off New Zealand, fly-rod-toting travelers have discovered the huge schools of kahawai (Australian salmon) that roam within a half mile (0.8 km) of the shore. Terrific catches have been made there only in the past decade.

A quick review of the existing saltwater fly records shows that about one third of the marks have been set in the past ten years: that's proof that this record category is rapidly evolving. But you don't have to travel half-way around the world to get your shot at a record. There are abundant opportunities stateside, too, even in traditional fly-fishing haunts such as the Florida Keys. Old-timers complain about the crowds and expensive charters, but this hotbed of angling activity—with over 30 species of fish locally—is still a major locale in the world of record fishing.

As in conventional line-class categories, the secret to catching a record fish on fly has much to do with being in the right place at the right time. These days, many crews in the most prolific fishing ports are trained in the latest techniques and IGFA rules. Supply and demand has forced these professionals to diversify and to keep up with trends, but the demand also indicates that the record-hunting competition is getting tougher. How can you increase your chances of succeeding in a record pursuit?

Tackle Selection

One way is to start with the right equipment. Consider rods first.

Fly rod selection starts with line weight selection. Anglers with a lot of coastal fishing

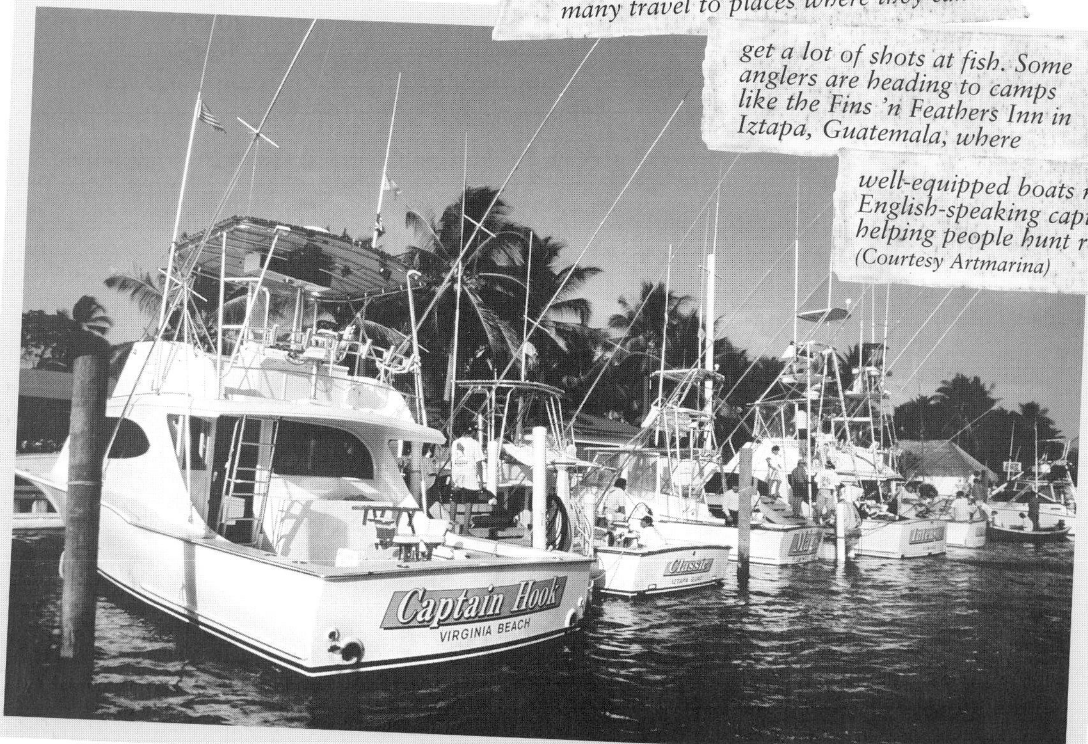

These days, record fishermen are discovering the thrill of targeting billfish on fly. To perfect their technique, many travel to places where they can get a lot of shots at fish. Some anglers are heading to camps like the Fins 'n Feathers Inn in Iztapa, Guatemala, where well-equipped boats manned by English-speaking captains are helping people hunt records. (Courtesy Artmarina)

"In saltwater fly-fishing, you don't have to worry about casting very far. But you have to be able to wind fast and vigorously. If you cast with your right hand, wind with your right, even if you are accustomed to winding with your left . . . to increase the speed of your retrieve."

—Stu Apte, 44+ records

experience say the best all-around line weight for fish under 50 pounds (22.6 kg) is 9 or 10 (4 or 4.5 kg). And if you have to choose just one as a do-all, it should be a 9 weight. However, a better-than-average caster might get by with an 8 (3.6 kg), and there are times when the added weight of a 10 is an advantage in heavy wind. For ambitious anglers targeting the dream fish, like big tarpon or even billfish, 12- or 13-weight (5.4 or 5.85 kg) rods can do the job, although few experts recommend anything larger.

The trend toward catching bigger fish on fly has driven advancements in this piece of artillery. If you have an amberjack, tarpon, or tuna down deep, the only way to bring the fish up to the boat is by physically lifting it with the line and rod. Freshwater rods don't need this muscle. Lifting power is a consideration that's unique to salt water. A shorter rod yields more leverage—or lifting power—to use against the fish. For the average angler, a rod from 8 feet, 6 inches to 9 feet, 6 inches (2.6 m to 2.9 m) is a good compromise for most fishing situations, with 9 feet (2.75 m) as a good average. You can fish longer rods, but their downside is that the additional length can slow your presentation. And in sight-fishing for world records, getting the fly to your prey quickly is crucial.

As for reels, the two types most commonly used by record-seeking anglers today are the anti-reverse, which won't revolve backward, and the direct-drive reel. There's also a third reel that's referred to as a multiplying type. Because this reel picks up line faster (one revolution on the reel handle turns two or more revolutions of the spool), it's popular among those who can't wind quickly. However, this reel is off-limits to record-seeking anglers. The IGFA won't consider a fish caught on a multiplying reel; in fact, some light-tackle clubs and tournaments frown on its use, too.

Reel drag doesn't always mean much in many freshwater applications, but it's helpful in most saltwater situations. In most fishing conditions, you will want less than a pound (0.45 kg) of drag, and it's necessary only when the fish first takes the line. After that, less mechanical drag is required; skilled anglers use their fingers and hands to apply necessary pressure. What's critical, however, is that the drag release the line smoothly. A leader can break easily if it's jerked suddenly. If the drag is smooth throughout the first few pounds of adjustment, it will serve you well. Backing is an important consideration when choosing a fly reel for record fishing, too. Many experienced saltwater anglers believe the minimum capacity for any size reel should be no less than 200 yards (180 m) of Dacron backing plus the full fly line.

"Paper records. That's what anglers call marks that are too easy."

Access Approachable Records

Experts agree that a number of species in various tippet categories could be toppled by anglers with adequate ability, although luck will sometimes play a hand in your success. The trick is to identify the fish you think you can handle and then plan a strategy from there.

Jim Chapralis, a fly angler and president of Pan Angling, an adventure travel service, pointed out records listed in the 1998 edition of *World Record Game Fishes* that could be broken with forethought and diligence. "In the men's category, the cubera snapper is wide open except for the 16-pound [8 kg] tippet, and it's completely vacant for women. It would be possible to get a few records on this one species in a single trip. You just have to locate a place where cubera snapper congregate."

There are other record-breaking opportunities in the relatively new 20-pound (10 kg) tippet class category for men, says Chapralis. Sizes for a number of species in this class are just average. Tripletail, for instance. The 20-pound (10 kg) tippet record is now 16 pounds, 6 ounces (7.42 kg), which is 4 pounds (1.81 kg) less than the 16-pound-tippet (8 kg) class record. The spotted seatrout record on 20 is 6 pounds, 8 ounces (2.94 kg), but that's almost 6 pounds (2.7 kg) less than the current 16-pound-tippet mark. Then there's striped bass. At 33 pounds (14.96 kg), the 20-pound (10 kg) record is a whopping 18 pounds (8.16 kg) lighter than the 16-pound (8 kg) tippet record, and over 30 pounds (13.6 kg) lighter than the fish caught on 12-pound (6 kg), which is 64 pounds, 8 ounces (29.25 kg).

Del Brown holds three of the most difficult saltwater fly records: the 2-, 4-, and 8-pound (1, 2, and 4 kg) tippet class marks for permit.

This fast, tough-fighting fish has a mouth as tough as shoe leather and is the ultimate challenge for saltwater fly-rodders. (Courtesy Del Brown)

> *"There's no justification for fishing 20, unless you're fishing big game, like marlin. But to have that tippet class for something like bluegill? That's ridiculous. Why bother with a tippet that tests higher than the weight of the fish?"*
>
> —Del Brown

Opportunities exist on 20 (10 kg), but one complaint you hear occasionally from fly fishing veterans is that 20 isn't worth pursuing since it's not sporting. Says Del Brown, who currently holds three exceptional records for permit on fly: "There's no justification for fishing 20, unless you're fishing big game, like marlin. But to have that tippet class for something like bluegill? That's ridiculous. Why bother with a tippet that tests higher than the weight of the fish?"

Paper records. That's what captains and anglers will call marks that are far from challenging. However, what some call "too easy" a less-experienced angler may call "hard work." What some anglers call a paper record could be good practice for amateurs still struggling to get their sea legs in the sport of saltwater fly-fishing.

When assessing appropriate records for your skill level, check out the vacant listings. More than two thirds of the women's saltwater fly records are vacant, and there are a few available for men, too. Stephen Sloan, an IGFA trustee, founder of the radio program "Fishin' Zone," and a New York–based angler with 44 records to his credit (18 still stand), references the 2-, 4-, and 6-pound (1, 2, and 3 kg) tippet vacancies for albacore. Nabbing the marks on this species—considered an excellent light-tackle fish—would be a tough feat, but it's doable, he says. His strategy? He would head to the Hudson Canyon off New Jersey, where the 20-pound (10 kg) tippet record was set, in late August or September, when this species makes seasonal migrations into colder waters. "You could get lucky and be there on a day when they're buzzing around."

However, just because a record is vacant doesn't mean it's attainable. For instance, there are currently no records standing for Atlantic halibut, but those marks could remain vacant for a long time. Commercial overfishing has taken a big toll on the numbers of this deep-swimming species.

When reviewing the *World Record Game Fishes* for your fly-fishing-record conquest, keep one other thing in mind. "Fish for pleasure first and let the record thing be secondary," says Del Brown. "I've seen people become obsessed with that goal, and have it kill their interest in the actual fishing. Fish for fun, but to increase your odds of obtaining a record, set up according to IGFA rules."

The New Frontier: Billfish on Fly

When pioneers like Stu Apte, Lee Cuddy (who caught the first Atlantic sailfish on fly), and Winston Moore (who has caught more than 100 billfish on fly) were stretching the limits of their gear on the likes of billfish back in the 1960s, they probably didn't realize that their experimental efforts were laying the groundwork for what is now one of the most talked-about forms of fly fishing. Today, enterprising anglers continue to make fantastic catches, the type few would have dreamed possible years ago.

Teasing 101

BIG-GAME RECORD-SEEKING anglers owe a lot to Webster Robinson. Prior to his discovery of how to take billfish on fly, these species were considered beyond the realm of this tackle. Today, the technique he pioneered is used by crews around the world in attempts to help anglers take trophy-size fish.

In *Fly FIshing in Salt Water*, Lefty Kreh writes about the time Robinson was fishing in Panama for black marlin with his wife Helen and Captain Louis Schmidt when he became frustrated by the scores of sailfish that were attacking his baits. So he fashioned a wooden plug without hooks and trolled it behind the boat near the marlin baits in the hope that the sailfish would attack it, instead. That's when he discovered how aggressive sails can be. When the hookless wooden lure was reeled in, the fish would continue to attack the lure. Often, the sails were so intent upon killing and eating the wooden lure that they remained within a few feet of the transom.

This behavior prompted Robinson to consider fly-fishing for sails. He went home to Key West, Florida, to devise a sporting strategy, one that would conform to the regulations of his home club, the Rod and Reel Club of Miami Beach. Those regulations called for a leader with a breaking strength of 12 pounds (6 kg) and a shock leader attached to the fly that did not exceed 1 foot (0.3 m) (the IGFA adheres to these rules today).

On January 18, 1962, Webster stood on the deck of the *Caiman*, with Schmidt at the helm, while Helen held a trolling rod. Skipping in the wake behind the boat was a strip of bonito belly that had been cut and sewn to resemble a fish. The bait, which replaced the wooden plug, was hookless.

When sailfish rose behind the skipping bait, Helen fed a little line back so the sail got a good taste of the bait. Then she jerked the bonito away and reeled it closer to the boat. Enraged, the angry fish moved forward. The process was repeated several times, until the fish was within casting range. That's when Schmidt put the boat in neutral. Helen removed the teaser bait and Webster made a legal cast with a white popping bug. He popped the bug to attract the sail, then raised the rod so the fly could skitter on the surface. The fish came forward and buried the bait with his bill. Forty minutes later, the 74-pound (33.5 kg) sailfish was ready to be boated.

The bonito belly was a factor in Webster Robinson's success. In fact, many experts today believe natural bait is superior to artificial teasers. Webster eventually captured 14 more Pacific sailfish and later employed his teasing method on striped marlin, which are even harder to excite than sails. He took history's first marlin on a fly rod. The marlin weighed 145 pounds (65.77 kg).

Most recently, the IGFA received its first application for a broadbill swordfish taken on fly. The 54-pound, 10-ounce (24.76 kg) fish was caught along the Kenyan coast in April 1998 by angler Jeremy Block on the charter boat *Eclare* with Richard Moller at the helm. Prior to news of this catch, many anglers and captains believed no person would lure this species to a fly. Swordfish are finicky, are easily frightened by an approaching boat, and rarely strike blindly. Typically, the bait must be presented carefully and

> *"When a hook gets moved back and forth in this fish's mouth, it has a tendency to slide out. . . . It can be heartbreaking."*
>
> —R. T. Trosset, 100+ records

repeatedly before the swordfish will consider it, and the slashing bill can make short work of an angler's line or leader. Nevertheless, Block employed some outstanding trickery to get this precocious fish interested in his fly, and 35 minutes later the swordfish was gaffed, although Moller noted the fish maintained its reputation as an ocean-going gladiator by fighting ferociously to the very end.

That pending record, along with existing records for billfish by the likes of legendary anglers such as Billy Pate, Charlie Tombras, and Jim Gray (who has two Pacific blue marlin over 200 pounds [90 kg]), have stoked the imaginations of veteran and amateur fly-rodders with a hankering for an exciting and inimitable challenge.

Fly-fishing legend Billy Pate caught this 86-pound (39.0 kg) Atlantic sailfish on 16-pound (8 kg) tippet.

Unlike shallow-water fishing, where a silent approach is generally mandatory and casting must be done with care, the emphasis in deepwater angling for billfish is on locating a fish and then getting something in front of it for it to strike. Webster Robinson pioneered the teasing method being used successfully today (see "Teasing 101," page 61). Can an amateur perfect the necessary techniques and vie for a record?

The odds are good, says Stu Apte, who teaches fly-fishing for billfish in the sailfish meccas of Central America, in places such as Costa Rica, Guatemala, and Panama. "I've taught people who've already had record fish on." Apte, a former airline pilot and Florida Keys guide with over 44 records to his credit, says his dream is to help one of his students break a standing record of his own. A good species to fine-tune techniques on is sailfish. To land this electric fighter on fly successfully, he says, anglers should concentrate on learning how to pick up line quickly.

"In this type of fishing, you don't have to worry about casting very far. But you have to be able to wind fast and vigorously. If you cast with your right hand, wind with your right, even if you are accustomed to winding with your left. This technique can increase the speed of your retrieve." A fast retrieve is crucial in this type of fishing, since it's easier to put more pressure on a fish when it's closer to the boat.

Whether you choose to charter a boat in a billfish-rich area or run your own vessel with

Work Your Boat

THE BOAT YOU fly fish from is crucial for success when targeting records in salt water. It will get you within range of your quarry and is your casting platform once there. Whether you fish from a flats-style rig in the shallows for tarpon, or from conventional offshore wagons for deep-water pelagic species, you should use your boat as efficiently as you use tackle. Following are ways to do that.

1. Loose gear, including anchors, ropes and tackle boxes, should be stored away from the range of your casts, and windshields should be eliminated or folded down to offer more area for casting. Keep the cockpit or casting platform free of line-entangling items. If you drop loose coils of fly line on a deck that is obstructed, you could lose your chance at a record fish.

2. If your boat doesn't have a casting platform you may have problems handling the yards of fly line that spill onto the deck when retrieving. Some anglers place a large bucket beside their stripping hand and use it to deposit line into.

3. A crucial element of saltwater fly-fishing is spotting the fish and informing your crew of its exact location. Guides have worked out a system that makes that easy to do. It's called the clock technique, and in sightfishing, it's an effective way for the boat crew to keep tabs on the position of incoming fish. When standing in the boat, imagine it is a clockface. The end where the angler stands is always twelve o'clock; the other end is six o'clock. Nine o'clock is to the left of the angler, and three is to the right. Say you're on a shallow bar and the guide sees a bonefish tail above the surface. If he says "nine o'clock, 50 feet away" the angler will know to start making a cast to the left.

4. An important job for the captain is to maneuver the boat properly. The person casting should be in a position to cast downwind whenever possible. A fish 60 feet away in a 25-mph upwind breeze is safe from most fly anglers, but it's a reasonable target for someone casting downwind.

friends and family as crew, there's one rule that's sometimes overlooked by those pursuing fly records for billfish today: the engine or engines of the boat must be in neutral when the angler makes a cast. There are complaints that some crews abuse this regulation. Some are getting the fly into the

"The emphasis in deepwater angling for billfish is on locating a fish and then getting something in front of it for it to strike."

Strategic Planning

ALTHOUGH THE TREND in fly-fishing today is to cast long rods in salt water, some ocean anglers with a hankering for records are finding new opportunities in freshwater. While purist fly rodders continue to pursue the holy grail of freshwater—trout—others are going after less conventional species. One person is Herb Ratner. This Pennsylvania native has over 77 records to his credit, including some awesome light tackle marks for tarpon and tiger shark, but this past year, he racked up a few records in freshwater on fly rod for an old favorite in the Northeast, rock bass. The strategy Ratner employed to earn those marks provides a good example for anyone to follow.

Having discovered that the fly records for rock bass were vacant, Ratner began his search for a local expert, a guide who could put him on to big numbers of this fish. He chose an old friend, Jeff Caputo of Pittsburgh, who had been fishing Lake Erie for over 10 years and knew which shores to scour for this species. Neither Ratner nor Caputo had ever caught a rock bass on fly, but they were committed to discovering the proper techniques.

In the summer of 1997, they took many car trips to Lake Erie, investing at least 150 hours casting along the south shore, trying different tackle and fly combinations, observing conditions and taking copious notes. In time, they discovered that concentrations of rock bass occur around rock piles in 3 to 8 feet (1 to 2.5 m) of water when temperatures are between 67° and 72°F (19° and 22°C). In addition, their odds of finding fish increased when the wind came from the West, and the sun was on the lake. After long days during which Ratner would cast as many as 300 times, this tenacious angling team also learned that this species will take yellow and white streamer flies. Equipped with this newfound knowledge, they caught their first rock bass record on fly that summer on a double-tapered 6-weight floating line and 8-foot leader.

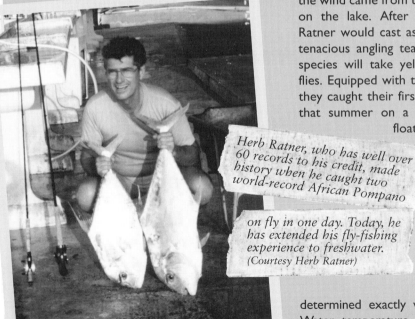

Herb Ratner, who has well over 60 records to his credit, made history when he caught two world-record African Pompano on fly in one day. Today, he has extended his fly-fishing experience to freshwater. (Courtesy Herb Ratner)

But one is not enough, particularly for record-obsessed anglers. In the spring of 1998, they planned another expedition to Erie. By reviewing the notes they had kept the year before, Ratner and Caputo determined exactly when and where to fish. Water temperature was (continued on next page)

Strategic Planning

continued from page 64

a key concern. "Temperatures in Erie can change overnight," says Caputo, 37. "Because the lake is shallow, waves can pound hard, and bury the warm water. When that happens, the fishing gets shut off." With a six-week window of opportunity the pair readied Caputo's 18-foot Alumacraft boat for their next mission. Ratner called me last August with an update: five more rock bass records on fly, which brings his total fly rod record tally to 39. Does that mean he's done with rock bass? Ratner says he's not quitting yet. "We're going back next week."

water and stripping line while the engines are still in gear. But remember, a fish hooked on a trolled fly is an *illegal catch*; in addition, it's not very sporting.

Many a great billfish has never made it into the record books because of rule infringements. One of the heartbreaking losses occurred when Californian Denton Hill caught a 174-pound (78.92 kg) striped marlin on 16-pound (8 kg) tippet class. It would have set a new world record had it not been subdued with a long-handled gaff with a detachable head. Although the head was securely wrapped with 100-pound (45 kg) monofilament line, the IGFA said it was a flying gaff, which is not permitted under the rules.

Experiment with a fly rod for billfish and you'll encounter some tough breaks and hard fighting. But that's half the fun of this sport.

> *"Sometimes you have to step back and just ward off blows when you're hurting. But then you have to go back in and finish it. That's how it is for boxing and light-tackle fishing."*
>
> —Stu Apte

Stu Apte, who used to box in his youth (he won the Miami Golden Gloves competition in 1947), compares this style of record fishing to long rounds in the ring. "Sometimes you have to step back and just ward off blows when you're hurting. But then you have to go back in and finish it. That's how it is for boxing and light-tackle fishing."

6

THE AMAZING HUNT FOR LARGEMOUTH BASS

Allan Cole has a recurring nightmare. He's fighting a lunker largemouth bass, a fish with a head the size of a football and a belly as thick as a suitcase. In the dream, he's aware that the hawg on his hook is bigger than the existing all-tackle record of 22 pounds, 4 ounces (10.09 kg), yet as he wrestles with the trophy-sized fish from the cockpit of a small boat he begins to feel anxious and tense, the same way many people do when having nightmares about being chased or stalked. The anxiety gives way to panic as Cole starts to lose control of the fish. Then the bass shakes its giant head, spits the hook, and turns on its hefty side before waving good-bye with its tail fin. "When it disappears, it's as if I've been struck in the heart with an ice pick," he says. This 56-year-old painting contractor and lure designer has been enduring that nightmare ever since he lost a real trophy bass in California's Lake Castaic in the early 1980s.

A heartbreaking loss has the power to haunt an angler, particularly when the one that gets away is a potential world-record largemouth bass. More than any other freshwater fish, the largemouth records—the all-tackle mark in particular—fascinate many of the 30 million bass anglers nationwide. It's easy to see why: for starters, the standing all-tackle fish is one of the oldest and most prestigious records in the IGFA book. It's a controversial record, too, and one of the toughest to beat. And, by the way, the person who breaks the standing mark has an outside chance of becoming a millionaire. Now you understand why anglers worldwide find this record alluring.

It's feasible to break the all-tackle largemouth bass record, although you should know about the competition: anglers targeting this record have been at it for decades, and this highly strategic group is also highly suspicious of trophy claims.

In January 1993, while trolling the 12-inch (30 cm) AC Plug that he designed, Cole hooked and lost what he estimates to have been a 23- to 25-pound (10.43 to 11.33 kg) largemouth. Cole, who has a number of big fish to his credit, realizes that few anglers come face to fin with a largemouth of that size in their lifetimes. "Most people don't get a chance at a bass like that. I had one, but I lost it. Now I have these bad dreams because I'm not sure I'll ever get another shot at one."

Anglers are still talking about the late George Perry, dubbed the Babe Ruth of bass fishing, and the all-tackle fish he caught over six decades ago. No pictures of his amazing 22-pound, 4-ounce (10.06 kg) fish exist, but Perry has been photographed with other large bass, including this 13-pound, 14-ounce (6.30 kg) fish he caught in 1934. (Courtesy Bill Baab)

The Largest Bass of All Time

Cole is one of countless bass anglers who pursue the all-tackle record, which was set back in 1932. The record-setting angler, George Perry, became the Babe Ruth of bass fishing when he caught the 22-pound, 4-ounce (10.06 kg) largemouth that would become fishing's Holy Grail. The story of Perry's world-record catch has probably been told more times than Roland Martin has cast a crankbait, with the expected result that many of the story's facts have been garbled over the decades. Even so, the basic details of one of record fishing's oldest tales and most famous fish are not as spectacular as you might think.

Top 25 Bass of All Time

EVER WONDER WHY so many avid largemouth bass anglers say the next all-tackle record will come out of the state of California? The answer could be found in this list of the largest largemouth of all time. Compiled by Bart Crabb, author of *The Quest for the World Record Bass*, this all-star list represents documented catches, those caught according to state regulations and certified upon weighing. (Only a few made the IGFA record book, namely the Crupi and Kadota catches.) Of the fish listed here, 21 were plucked from California lakes. But that doesn't mean you can figure the odds in this record-fishing game. Unpredictable things can happen. For instance, the 18-pound, 14-ounce (8.25 kg) largemouth record was taken in Lake Isabella on—of all things—a Zebco 202. To top it off, Keith Harper was fishing from shore with a broken-tip rod when he caught it. He was 12 years old at the time, and his father was fishing the lake for the big ones.

No.	Weight, lb.-oz. (kg)	Angler	Date	Catch Location
1.	22-4 (10.06)	George Perry	6/2/1932	Montgomery Lake, GA
2.	22-01 (10)	Bob Crupi	3/12/1991	Lake Castaic, CA
3.	21-12 (9.84)	Mike Aurjo	3/5/1991	Lake Castaic, CA
4.	21-3 (9.57)	Ray Easley	3/4/1980	Lake Casitas, CA
5.	21-0 (9.52)	Bob Crupi	3/9/1990	Lake Castaic, CA
6.	20-15 (9.48)	Dave Zimmerlee	6/23/1973	Lake Miramar, CA
7.	20-13.7 (9.43)	Leo Torres	2/4/1990	Lake Castaic, CA
8.	20-4 (9.16)	Gene Dupras	5/26/1985	Lake Hodges, CA
9.	20-2 (9.11)	Fritz Friebel	5/19/1923	Big Fish Lake, FL
10.	20-0 (9.07)	Phil Jay	6/21/1977	Lake Miramar, CA
11.	19-10 (8.89)	Bruce Newsome	1/17/1993	Baccarrac, Mexico
12.	19-8 (8.84)	Keith Gunsauls	3/1/1988	Lake Miramar, CA
13.	19-4 (8.70)	Chris Brandt	3/21/1998	Lake Miramar, CA
14.	19-3 (8.66)	Arden Hanline	2/15/1987	Morena Lake, CA
15.	19-3 (8.66)	Steve Beasly	2/3/1986	Lake Wohlford, CA
16.	19-1.5 (8.64)	Sandy DeFresco	3/14/1988	Lake Miramar, CA
17.	19-0.4 (8.63)	Dan Kadota	1/8/1989	Lake Castaic, CA
18.	18-14 (8.57)	Keith Harper	4/7/1984	Lake Isabella, CA
19.	18-13 (8.52)	Joe Weaver	2/5/1984	Lake Isabella, CA
20.	18-12.9 (8.50)	Bud Wright	4/12/1987	St. Johns River, FL
21.	18-12 (8.48)	Bob Eberly	3/9/1980	Lower Otay, CA
22.	18-12 (8.48)	Jim Steurgeon	2/26/1981	San Vicente, CA
23.	18-12 (8.48)	Dan Kadota	2/12/1988	Lake Castaic, CA
24.	18-12 (8.48)	Manny Aurjo	1/25/1991	Lake Castaic, CA
25.	18-11 (8.43)	Bill Beckum	1/15/1980	Lake Casitas, CA

"Live baits tell me what's going on under the water. They react differently when fish are on the spot."

—Dan Kadota, 1 IGFA bass record

In 1932, Perry was a 19-year-old farmer and provider for his family following the death of his father the year before. Perry worked hard to keep food on the table during those tough days of the Great Depression. But on June 2, a driving rain forced him to surrender a day's work in his fields near the town of Helena, Georgia. Perry went fishing, instead. He did so for fun and also with the hope that he could hook something for dinner. He cast a line from the small, homemade jonboat he kept on Montgomery Lake, an oxbow off the Ocmulgee River in Telfair County.

"I don't remember many details," Perry told outdoor writer Vic Dunaway of *Sports Afield* (May 1969). "But all at once the water splashed everywhere. I do remember striking, then rearing back and trying to reel, but nothing budged. I thought for sure I'd lost the fish, that he had dived and hung me up. I had no idea how big it was, but that didn't matter. What had me worried was losing the lure." At that time, Perry rarely fished with more than one artificial, since money for lures took a long time to save. (According to Bill Baab, outdoor editor of the *Augusta Chronicle* and a George Perry historian, the angler was fishing with a Wiggle Fish lure in perch scale, manufactured by the Creek Chub Bait Company.)

Once he had boated the bass, Perry, like any proud angler, took it to a general store to show it to his friends. That's when someone told him about the Big Fish Contest sponsored by *Field & Stream* magazine. Locals urged him to enter. He had the fish measured and weighed on a set of certified scales in the post office, and he had a witness notarize the information, all according to contest rules. Having taken care of formalities, Perry picked up his fish and brought it back home. That night, his mother, Rubye, fried one side of the largest largemouth documented in history and served it up for supper with onions, tomatoes, and cornbread.

Weeks later, a new rod and reel arrived at the Perry farm. The equipment was part of a $75 prize awarded to George from the *Field & Stream* contest sponsors.

So how did Perry's record make it into the IGFA book? In 1978, the magazine transferred all of its freshwater records and record-keeping responsibilities to the IGFA. Perry's fish was automatically granted IGFA record status, even though it hadn't been certified by modern rules, which today specify that photos must be taken of trophy fish. Because there were no photographs of this all-tackle record and because the contest records are missing, too, there is no concrete evidence of the catch. As a result, bass anglers nationwide

"On lakes, many people have no idea what's going on underneath the boat. But if you know which way the current is going, you'll know which way the fish is facing and how to present the bait."

—Dan Kadota

hotly debate whether a fish this size ever really existed. The controversy is fired by the fact that no one has been able to beat the record. Sixty-six years have passed as swiftly as current over eel grass, and as time goes by, Perry and his fish acquire the status of legend and myth.

Some say Perry's catch was a fluke. But that 19-year-old farm boy, who died in a plane crash at the age of 61, proved himself to be a skilled angler two years later, when he caught another big bass (13 pounds, 14 ounces [6.30 kg]) to win a 1934 *Field & Stream* contest. Perry, it seems, had the personality traits of a true record angler. He was methodical and persistent in his hobby, and also in his business. Even though he had a sixth-grade education, Perry eventually became a pilot and entrepreneur, leasing and operating the Municipal Airport in Brunswick, Georgia. As with so many of the anglers who are successfully capturing multiple records today, Perry's determination and persistence won him success personally and professionally. Yet those who knew him say he remained a modest man, particularly about his phenomenal bass.

Methodical anglers who have made attempts to break Perry's record have explored the details of his catch in the hopes that it can be emulated, particularly the location of the catch. But Perry long ago discounted the possibility that Montgomery Lake could harbor another record. "It's been filling in ever since," he said in the *Sports Afield* article. "Now it's pretty shallow and weedy. I'm afraid there's not much in my story that could help anyone catch a new record. I wish luck to anyone who wants to try, but I won't make any prediction. It seems to me there just aren't as many big fish as there used to be."

"Most people don't get a chance at a bass like that. I had one, but I lost it. Now I have these bad dreams because I'm not sure I'll ever get another shot at one."

—Allan Cole, dedicated bass angler

Where Are the Last of the Big Fish?

Was Perry right when he conjectured that largemouth bass of bygone days grew to greater sizes than they do now? Not likely, say the experts. In fact, more truly large bass—those over 18 pounds (8.16 kg)—have been caught in the last two decades than have ever been recorded. The reason for the increase in numbers of big bass has a lot to do with advances in fisheries biology, management, and the weird science of transplantational genetics.

Experts hypothesize that Perry's fantastic fish was not a freak of nature. It was probably produced when a northern largemouth bred with a Florida subspecies. Today, that cross-breeding occurs artificially in many states throughout the country, thanks to stocking programs. As a result, state records have fallen like dominoes. Of the 49 states that support largemouth bass, 37 set recent records since 1970; only 6 states have record bass predating 1960.

The good news for record hunters is that stocking programs are getting more aggressive as local governments recognize the recreational value of the shadowy, temperamental bass. One reason: the largemouth is the most sought-after gamefish in the world. In the U.S. alone, there are over 30 million bass anglers, and a $40 billion industry has grown

Where to go for a trophy bass? Some say California's Lake Castaic is the place to be. This body of water rocked the bass fishing world from 1989 to 1992, when four line-class records were taken here. One of those records was this 17-pound, 1 ounce (7.76 kg) lunker caught by Robert J. Crupi in 1990.

up around their needs, according to the Bass Anglers Sportsmen Society (B.A.S.S.).

Since Perry's 22-pound, 4-ounce (10.09 kg) fish, only eight bass over 20 pounds (9 kg) have been recorded, and each came from the same state: California. The largest of those fish was a 22-pounder, but those who scour the local waters for records say they've seen largemouth to rival that hawg. That's one reason the anglers who are seriously targeting this all-tackle record predict that it will be broken in California.

In Search of the All-Tackle Record

Many people associate California with sunshine and celebrities, but for anglers, the state is well known for the bodies of water that are producing famously fat largemouth bass.

According to Bart Crabb, largemouth mania began in 1973, when San Diego's Lake Miramar gave up a 20-pound, 15-ounce (9.48 kg) Florida-strain bass to Dave Zimmerlee on June 23. "Zimmerlee and his bass brought instant fame and recognition to the lake and the state of California. His catch gave hope to a lot of anglers who wanted to be the proud owners of the record, and it almost started a stampede to southern California much like the Gold Rush days."

Twenty-five years later, fish weighing in the teens have been caught regularly, along with an occasional 20-pounder (9 kg). These big fish keep alive California's dreams of securing the next world record.

How Big Can a Largemouth Get?

There's no secret to producing trophy-sized largemouth. California's success with bass is based on the fact that the state has introduced the Florida-strain largemouth (which is physically longer than other subspecies) into areas that encourage the fish to grow to its largest, gill-shaking potential. Among the necessary elements are a long growing season, diversified structure, and deep-water access. But many bodies of water in the United States have those things.

What's special about California is its rainbow trout. These easy-to-catch prey, which the state stocks in generous numbers, are the ideal forage for largemouth bass. Rainbow trout are rich in protein, allowing bass to grow very big in a short period of time, acting like a natural steroid. The presence of trout as a forage base in California will make it very difficult for other states—including the bass powerhouses of Texas and Florida—to produce megaheavy largemouths.

However, raising trophy-sized fish is a tricky science. For instance, the hottest areas in California that have produced the biggest fish in recent years could be on the decline. One example is Lake Castaic, which rocked the bass fishing world from 1989 to 1992 with four IGFA line-class records in four consecutive years. The largest catch from this modestly sized man-made lake was a whopping 22-pounder (10 kg) hooked by Robert J. Crupi in 1991, a policeman. That same year, Mike Aurjo took a 21-pound, 12-ounce (9.84 kg) catch and Leo Torres wrestled in a 20-pound, 13-ounce (9.43 kg) largemouth. Today, some anglers say this hotbed of activity could be on the decline. Where will all the lunkers go? Here's one theory:

Lake Castaic was filled in 1971, and Florida-strain fish were put in the lake in the mid-1970s. These fish had virtually no competition for food, so the growth potential was high. Since bass are often at their peak weights between the ages of 11 and 13 years, it seems the headline-making fish of the late 1980s and early 1990s represented mature bass from that first-generation of Florida-strain fish. But according to scientists, future generations rarely grow as big as the first one.

In addition to mother nature, there's another force fighting against the development of trophy-sized largemouth: fishing pressure. On Lake Castaic, for instance, the competition among anglers was intense following Crupi's 22-pounder (10 kg). Angler Porter Hall of Ventura, California, recalls that anglers would park overnight near the lake in order to be the first ones out fishing in the morning. "The lake is only about 25 acres, yet there would be as many as 300 boats out there. People would fight and argue. It wasn't what you think of as fishing; it wasn't relaxing."

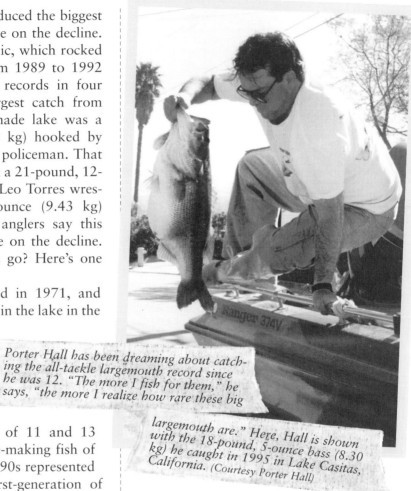

Porter Hall has been dreaming about catching the all-tackle largemouth record since he was 12. "The more I fish for them," he says, "the more I realize how rare these big largemouth are." Here, Hall is shown with the 18-pound, 5-ounce bass (8.30 kg) he caught in 1995 in Lake Casitas, California. (Courtesy Porter Hall)

Hall is a 43-year-old private investor who sold his house in Florida and moved to California in 1991 strictly to pursue bass fishing. Hall has dreamed of catching the all-tackle record largemouth since he took his first 10-pound (4.5 kg) bass in Alabama at the age of 12. "I don't know what it was about that fish—it just thrilled me. The more I fish for them, the more I realize how rare these big largemouth are. There's a certain beauty about them."

"I've learned to look for structure on structure, such as a point of land with a tree or rock on it. Trophy-sized bass search for foot at these locations."

—Dan Kadota

During his most intense period of fishing, Hall was targeting only trophy largemouth five days a week. To date, the closest he's come to attaining his dream has been an 18-pound, 5-ounce (8.3 kg) bass he caught in February 1995 in Lake Casitas, which lies north of Los Angeles and is a top pick for anglers targeting records today. Ray Easeley's 21-pound, 3-ounce (9.57 kg) bass was pulled from there in 1981.

Like many of his peers, Hall thinks the next all-tackle record is now swimming somewhere in California, despite the fishing pressure and cycles in lakes. If the fish isn't in Lake Casitas, Lake Castaic, or Castaic Lagoon, it could be farther north, where some giant fish are rumored to be swimming, including the 24-pounder (10.8 kg) that Paul Duclos says he weighed on a bathroom scale before releasing (see chapter 2).

Although many serious fishermen question the validity of Duclos's story, some bass veterans believe he really had a world-class fish on the line. One of them is Dan Kadota, a former charter-boat captain and the holder of the 20-pound (10 kg) line-class largemouth record: Kadota pulled a 19-pound (8.62 kg) fish from Lake Castaic in 1989. "Paul is one of the few anglers in northern California pursuing trophy fish. It's not a fly-by-night thing for him. He's had 15-pounders [6.8 kg] before that one. He's serious about it." In fact, it's the Duclos catch from Spring Lake near Santa Rosa that has Kadota betting the next all-tackle record will come out of northern California. "There's less fishing pressure there and more opportunity to catch big fish." To emphasize the potential of those northern waters, Kadota uses this example: "I've caught 103 largemouth over 10 pounds since I started targeting that species in the late 1960s. If I were to spend just one full year fishing in the north, I could match that number."

If you were to look at the world-record hunt through the cold and calculating eyes of a Las Vegas bookmaker, California is the odds-on favorite. But, remember, this record business only hinges on one fish, which means there's hope for those who are casting lines in other parts of the country. The best advice for these anglers?

Dan Kadota holds the 20-pound (10 kg) line class record for largemouth bass. It weighs 19 pounds (8.63 kg) and was caught in Lake Castaic.

Trophy-Bass Technique Tips

WHAT ARE THE techniques that today's West Coast pros are using to target trophy bass? To find out, we asked IGFA record holder Dan Kadota of California.

1 "In my mind, the single most important aspect of trophy bass fishing is current," says Kadota, which is something he learned from his experience as a saltwater skipper. If you can determine the direction of the current—which almost all reservoirs have—you can use it to take bait into the strike zone. When fishing for big mouth aboard a bass boat, the best way to assess what the current is doing is to double anchor, which holds the boat rock steady as the wind and current whip around it.

"Say I want to fish a spot where there's a tree on a point in 24 feet [7.3 m] of water. I'll run over the spot, and into 12 feet [3.7 m] of water. That's where I'll drop my marker and anchor." Other anglers, says Kadota, make the mistake of dropping their markers right on the fish at 24 feet, but that can spook the bass. "I cast from a distance, and let the current take the bait to the fish." The distance is determined by conditions; if it's windy he'll anchor farther away.

Double anchoring offers other benefits. One is improved bait presentation. "Trophy fish are most often caught in cooler water, when the metabolism of baitfish—as well as bass—is slower. If you're fishing from a boat with a trolling motor and you're not double anchored, the wind and current are moving the platform around, which means your baits could be screaming through water. In reality, the bait should be crawling, since it's so cold. That's why you have to set those anchors tight and slowly walk the crayfish to the bass. Remember, bass don't get to be trophy-sized if they're stupid," says Kadota. "They know how a bait is supposed to react."

2 Choose the right bait. "A natural presentation is critical if you want to catch large bass," says Kadota. "Fish don't get big by eating wood and plastics. That's why I use natural baits. Most of my big fish have come on crayfish. I've also caught a few nice fish with water dogs and mudsuckers." But that doesn't mean Kadota fishes only live bait. Like many trophy bass hunters, he recognizes the value of big artificials, those between 8 and 12 inches (20 and 30 cm). Each time he leaves the dock, he takes along a surface bait—the Castaic Trout by the Castaic Bait Co. is most popular in his area—plus subsurface artificials with lead heads. He has worked both live and artificial baits simultaneously, but he focuses on really working his live baits. "Live baits tell me what's going on under the water. They react differently when fish are on the spot." In fact, Kadota relies on the messages he receives from live bait to tell him when he should leave a spot. If the live baits are swimming calmly, he finds a new place to fish: *(continued on next page)*

Trophy-Bass Technique Tips

continued from page 75

when predator bass are on the scene, live baits twitch nervously at the end of the line.

3 Practice, practice. When it comes to record-fishing success, "there's no substitute for time on the water," Kadota says. He fishes as often as he can to learn what happens in the lake at different water levels. And he networks constantly with friends who fish in the area, collecting any insider information that's available. "I've learned to look for structure on structure, such as a point of land with a tree or rock on it. Trophy-sized bass search for food at those locations."

"A natural presentation is critical if you want to catch large bass. . . . Fish don't get big by eating wood and plastics. That's why I use natural baits."

—Dan Kadota

According to author Bart Crabb, the key is to look for lakes that have been stocked with Florida-strain largemouth bass in the last ten years. He uses Lake Pickthorne in Arkansas as an example. This rehabilitated lake was stocked with Florida largemouth in 1990. In 1997, the lake was already producing bass over 10 pounds (4.5 kg); fish in the teens could be taking baits soon. "When fishing for that elusive lunker, I advise you to carefully choose your body of water. The fisheries people in your state can help you find the right location. You could start by looking at those places that have produced 17- and 18-pounders [7.71 and 8.1 kg]. At the same time, keep an eye on those young lakes that are coming on fast, particularly ones establishing a new record every year."

Tips on Technique

There are probably only a few hundred anglers nationwide who are in search of a record hawg today. According to Kadota, they do it "for the enjoyment and challenge of catching a fish of that size and magnitude. Something that big has lived successfully. It doesn't make a lot of mistakes. It won't eat worms it has seen before. Big bass are smarter. But because of that, anglers who are seriously courting the all-tackle record will have to apply methods and techniques that aren't used frequently."

Kadota learned that lesson in 1989 when he earned his place in the record books. Unlike most of the anglers who were pursuing largemouth in Lake Castaic at that time, Kadota—who has an offshore fishing background—is well-versed in the effects of wind and current on fishing. "On lakes, many people have no idea what's going on underneath the boat. But if you know which way the current is going, you'll know which way the fish is facing and how to present the bait." To assess current, Kadota double-anchored his boat while fishing structure, then he presented live crayfish until the record fish bit his hook.

Today, Kadota is a representative for G. Loomis, a fishing tackle company. But before he signed on with that manufacturer, this angler—who also has an 18-pound, 12-ounce (8.48 kg) bass to his credit—was fishing anywhere from 240 to 300 days a year. He split his time between freshwater pursuits and offshore excursions on the charter boat he ran. "I'd fish from three to seven days a week. I was almost untouchable, although I had my share of skunks. But that's what it takes. To attain a record, you have to be committed to putting a lot of time in on the water."

In addition, time has to be spent wisely, even if that means sacrificing a shot at catching smaller fish. "Trophy bass anglers employ techniques that can make for very slow fishing," says Porter Hall. "Many are using live bait or great big trout imitation plugs. As a result, you can go for days without catching a single fish. The average guy can't do that for long. He gets bored and heads to shallow water with a smaller lure. Serious anglers think that's wasting time. We'd rather get skunked than go messing around with little fish."

In many ways, bass anglers begin a calculated assault in the same way saltwater anglers do when pursuing records. The key step is to fish in areas where there are both larger than average fish and good record potential. If that area is far from your backyard, it's a good idea to hire a guide. Porter Hall figured that out when he first moved to California. "The fishing out west is so dramatically different than it is in Florida. I chose to teach myself, but I could have saved myself 100 days if I would have spent some time with a guide." Hall also recommends contacting local experts in the areas you choose to fish. "Try to find those people whose names you see in magazines. Many of them are nice and willing to share information."

One of the things that makes largemouth bass one of the most popular gamefish in America is the fact that you don't have to be earning six figures to make it a hobby. This is Everyone's sport. In fact, you don't even need a boat to do it, as demonstrated by the boy who caught an 18-pound, 14-ounce (8.57 kg) largemouth while casting from the shore of Lake Isabella in California a few years back. However, a sturdy rod and reel are essential for successful bass fishing. And to increase your chances of obtaining a record, be sure the line is fresh. Anglers like Kadota change it every day.

> *"I've caught 103 largemouth over 10 pounds (4.5 km) since I started targeting that species in the late 1960s. If I were to spend just one full year fishing in northern California, I could match that number."*
>
> —Dan Kadota

Fraudulent Practices

What are the chances that a largemouth bass heavier than George Perry's will ever be caught? Many anglers and authorities say the odds are surprisingly good. Among the attempts there have been numerous reports of some fantastic fish, including 25- and 30-pounders (11.33 and 13.6 kg). Yet for one reason or another, these catches haven't been authenticated. And often, the record claims are suspicious at best.

One person who received a lot of media attention was Otis Broom. In 1984, he claimed to have landed a bass that came within one ounce of the Perry world record. Yet when word of the catch leaked out and Broom was inundated with phone calls from reporters, he decided he didn't want the publicity. No one ever saw his fish, but Broom says he pulled his giant bass out of the cooler, took out his knife, carved the meat from the fish and popped it in the oven. His record claim was never substantiated. Five years later, Jim T. Smith Sr. claimed to have caught a 20-pound, 1-ounce (9.09 kg) bass from a pond in southern Georgia. Smith was trying to sell his story to the highest bidder when the fish was placed on a set of Wildlife Resources Division scales and weighed in at only 11 pounds, 11 ounces (5.29 kg).

Fraudulent claims to the trophy-sized bass became so common that in April 1997, *Sporting Classics* magazine spoofed the trend with an article that said: "Have you heard about the new world-record bass? It weighed about 25 pounds and was supposed to have been caught in South Carolina." As it turned out, the magazine story was an April Fool's joke, and the only "catch" was that it didn't let readers in on the joke until the next issue was published.

There are hundreds of stories like these, including reports of anglers who have stuffed lead, buckshot, and other compact heavy materials into fish before weighing. Such desperate antics have prompted people to try to come up with tamper-proof solutions. Ray Scott, founder of B.A.S.S. and publisher of *BASS* magazine, has suggested that all bass records be certified under the following rules:

1. the fish must be preserved and presented for official weighing,
2. the fish should be X-rayed, and
3. the record applicant should consent to a polygraph examination to verify the facts.

Although those requirements may seem severe, the fact is that the all-tackle record largemouth is more than your average fish: it's one of the most prestigious marks to beat. Says the IGFA's Mike Leech, "The person who breaks that old record will become very famous in the fishing world."

For that reason, those targeting this record need to pay strict attention to the rules. Witnesses will be key. In fact, many experts recommend that anglers targeting the largemouth make a point of not fishing alone. Or, if you like to fish solo, always cast your line near another person, someone who can verify your story if a record bass hits your lure. In addition, it would be wise to contact the Fish and Game Department immediately following a catch that appears to be a potential record. These officials can help take you through the proper certification process, step-by-step, from properly measuring the catch to finding certified scales for weighing.

The Million-Dollar Record

One of the reasons the IGFA is a stickler for details on largemouth record claims is because this fish could be worth a lot of money. Some experts feel that the next world-record largemouth bass could pay over $1 million to the person who catches it. In short, the angler who beats George Perry's mark could make his money through advertising contracts, promotions, photo, and story rights.

The bottom line is that big bass can mean big bucks. But some zealous anglers overlook the fact that no one is going to hand over a large lump sum in exchange for a lunker fish. The next George Perry is going to have to earn the money. Insiders say the angler has to be prepared to quit his or her job to go on the road to give seminars and represent manufacturers and bass fishermen nationwide.

"It may take you ten years of working hard to make that money," says Kadota, who earns his living as a tackle representative. In addition, a seven-figure income won't be offered to just anyone. Many insiders say the success of the next record holder will depend on his or her sense of professionalism and ability to speak in public.

Catch the world-record largemouth bass and fame and fortune could be yours. That's a compelling reason to get out there and start casting. Still, a number of the most dedicated anglers say celebrity doesn't motivate them to pursue this precarious fish. Some, like Porter Hall, enjoy the thrill of pursuing such a large and rare creature. Then there are people like Bill Baab. He's been writing and reading about the Perry catch for over three decades. His sentiments? "I hope it is broken someday soon. Why? Because a new record will give us all something new to talk about."

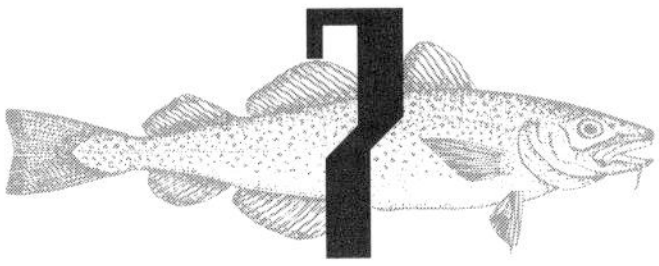

7 CHOOSING SALTWATER TACKLE

One of the liveliest debates about saltwater fishing is whether it's easier to catch world records today than it was when the IGFA was founded in 1939. When discussing inshore and offshore saltwater species, some will say "yes" and argue that increased commercial pressure has reduced the number of fish swimming in the oceans today, particularly the big ones. Trying to beat some of the old marks, they say, is a tough challenge, especially the all-tackle records for big-game that have been standing for years, such as Lou Marron's 1,182-pound (536.15 kg) swordfish caught off Chile in 1953. Yet others contend that improvements in the gear we use to find and fight fish provides today's angler with a considerable advantage.

Founding members of the IGFA were primarily wealthy big-game enthusiasts, with ready access to some of the best gear available for the recreational angler. Yet the tackle they used to battle the rugged giants of blue water, such as tuna and marlin, from open boats included reels with handles that spun backward when a hooked fish ran. Drag was exerted by applying thumb pressure against a leather tab that met the line, which was made of linen—a rough material that doesn't pull through water well and offers little stretch. These anglers came home with bloodied hands, busted knuckles, and broken fingers. For that reason, some of the fishing clubs for the well-to-do had surgeons on duty. Members of the most famous clubs, including the Tuna Club of Santa Catalina Island, were some of the first people to get their names in the IGFA record book, but not surprisingly, most of those marks have been beaten over the years by anglers fishing with improved gear and monofilament lines, which were developed after World War II.

According to Mike Farrier, president of the Tuna Club of Santa Catalina Island, and formerly the club's historian, today's gear is dramatically different from pre–World War II gear only in size and weight. Old reels were handcrafted with heavy materials. For instance, it was not uncommon for a big-game angler to fish with a reel that featured a sideplate measuring 8½ inches (22 cm). At

> *"The average angler isn't always aware of the subtle features that make for good quality fishing gear."*
>
> —Tommy Green, custom tackle outfitter

IGFA Equipment Regulations

FISHING FOR A world record means fishing with the appropriate tackle and terminal tackle. Following is a list of the gear that's either required or prohibited when targeting record fish (see also appendix, pages 113–15). See *World Record Game Fishes* for details on additional equipment, such as fighting chairs, gimbals, gaffs, nets, and rod belts. In addition to equipment rules, the book outlines angling rules, including actions that can disqualify a catch, such as changing the rod or reel while a fish is being played.

Rod

1 Rods must comply with sporting ethics and customs. Considerable latitude is allowed in the choice of a rod, but rods giving the angler an unfair advantage will be disqualified. This rule is intended to eliminate the use of unconventional rods.

2 The rod tip must be a minimum of 40 inches (101.6 cm) in length. The rod butt cannot exceed 27 inches (68.58 cm) in length. These measurements must be made from a point directly beneath the center of the reel. A curved butt is measured in a straight line. (The above measurements do not apply to surf-casting rods.)

Reel

1 Reels must comply with sporting ethics and customs.

2 Power-driven reels of any kind are prohibited. This includes motor, hydraulic, or electrically driven reels, and any device which gives the angler an unfair advantage.

3 Ratchet-handle reels are prohibited.

4 Reels designed to be cranked with both hands at the same time are prohibited.

Line

1 Monofilament, multifilament, and lead core multifilament lines may be used for all line classes, from 2- to 130-pound (1 to 60 kg) in salt water.

2 Wire lines are prohibited.

Line Backing

1 Backing not attached to the fishing line is permissible with no restrictions as to size or material.

2 If the fishing line is attached to the backing, the catch shall be classified under the heavier of the two lines. The backing may not exceed the 130-pound-line (60 kg) class and must be of a type approved for use in these angling rules.

Double Line

The use of a double line is not required. If one is used, it must meet the following specifications:

1 A double line must consist of the actual line used to catch the fish.

(continued on next page)

IGFA Equipment Regulations

continued from page 82

2 Double lines are measured from the start of the knot, braid, roll, or splice making the double to the furthermost end of the knot, splice, snap, swivel, or other device used for securing the trace, leader, lure, or hook to the double line.

In all line classes up to and including 20-pound (10 kg), the double line is limited to 15 feet (4.575 m). The combined length of the double line and leader cannot exceed 20 feet (6.1 m). The double line on all classes of tackle over 20-pound (10 kg) is limited to 30 feet (9.15 m). The combined length of the double line and leader cannot exceed 40 feet (12.2 m).

Leader

The use of a leader is not required. If one is used, it must meet the following specifications:

1 The length of the leader is the overall length including any lure, hook arrangement, or other device.

2 The leader must be connected to the line with a snap, knot, splice swivel, or other device. There are no regulations regarding the material or strength of the leader.

3 In all classes up to and including 20-pound (10 kg), the leader shall be limited to 15 feet (4.575 m). The combined length of the double line and leader shall not exceed 20 feet (6.1 m). The leader on all classes of tackle over 20-pound shall be limited to 30 feet (9.15 m). The combined length of the double line and leader shall be limited to 40 feet (12.2 m).

Hooks for Bait-Fishing

1 For live- or dead-bait fishing, no more than two single hooks may be used. Both must be firmly embedded in or securely attached to the bait. The eyes of the hooks must be no less than a hook's length apart and no more than 18 inches (45.72 cm) apart. The only exception is that the point of one hook may be passed through the eye of the other hook.

2 The use of a dangling or swinging hook is prohibited.

3 A two-hook rig for bottom fishing is acceptable if it consists of two single hooks on separate leaders or drops. Both hooks must be embedded in the respective baits and separated sufficiently so that a fish caught on one hook cannot be foul-hooked by the other.

4 All record applications made for fish caught on two-hook tackle must be accompanied by a photograph or a sketch of the hook arrangement.

Hooks and Lures

1 When using an artificial lure with a skirt or trailing material, no more than two single hooks *(continued on next page)*

IGFA Equipment Regulations

continued from page 83

may be attached to the line, leader, or trace. The hooks need not be attached separately. The eyes of the hooks must be no less than an overall hook's length apart and no more than 12 inches apart (30.48 cm). The only exception is that the point of one hook may be passed through the eye of the other hook. The trailing hook may not extend more than a hook's length beyond the skirt of the lure. A photograph or sketch showing the hook arrangement must accompany a record application.

2 Gang hooks are permitted when attached to plugs and other artificial lures that are specifically designed for this use. Gang hooks must be free swinging and shall be limited to a maximum of three hooks (either single, double, or treble, or a combination of any three). Baits may not be used with gang hooks. A photograph or sketch of the plug or lure must be submitted with record applications.

Compiled from regulations in the 1998 IGFA World Record Game Fishes

"I don't have the brute strength required for that type of fishing, but I do have stamina, which is necessary to catch trophy fish on light tackle."

—Jeanne DuVal, 50+ records

that time, offshore reels weighed as much as 30 pounds (13.5 kg). By comparison, today's big-game angler can do battle with smaller outfits—even bait-casting reels spooled with line under 12-pound (6 kg) test—and with gear that is manufactured with lightweight composite materials that are both durable and easy to handle.

Finding the Right Match

For saltwater anglers, today's gear is designed to help increase the odds of landing a record fish. The key to success, however, is to match tackle properly with your record fishing goals. This is a fact serious record hunters are well acquainted with, says Tommy Green, the owner of Custom Rod and Gun in Lighthouse Point, Florida. Unfortunately, amateur anglers aren't always as well educated.

Green's clients include all-star anglers such as Stewart Campbell and his captain, Barkey Garnsey, Kelly and Jocelyn Everett, Raleigh Werking and Pam Basco, serious anglers who travel the world for trophy fish and pack as many as a dozen rigs for a single fishing trip. These anglers know the importance of having the right equipment available if a larger than average fish is spotted off the transom. However, Green contends that you don't need an arsenal of saltwater equipment to take trophy fish. A savvy amateur can invest in one well-balanced rig and chase his record with it. The trick, says Green, is to target your species first and then match the tackle to that pursuit.

"Say some guy comes to me and says he wants to fish 16- or 20-pound [8 or 10 kg] test for tarpon. He may want to look at a spinning rod, but I'll tell him what I know about line twist on that type of gear. Then we'll discuss other options, maybe a conventional bait-caster, for what he's trying to do and where he plans to fish."

When selecting a rig, it can only help you to pick the brains of professionals. Green contends an amateur must collect information from as many knowledgeable sources as possible, particularly if big game is your target; it's the only way to stay competitive in a sport where there are a number of affluent anglers who can afford to travel the world and troll the most prolific waters, fine-tuning their theories on what type of gear is appropriate for certain situations. The average angler doesn't have a private boat with a full-time captain to consult with on tackle selection, but there are other reliable sources at the angler's disposal. You can learn a great deal about what is appropriate through magazine articles, advertisements, word of mouth, and from users or tackle shop recommendations. The latter should never be underestimated.

In Green's store, for instance, he has a staff of five employees who are qualified to answer questions about any type of fishing,

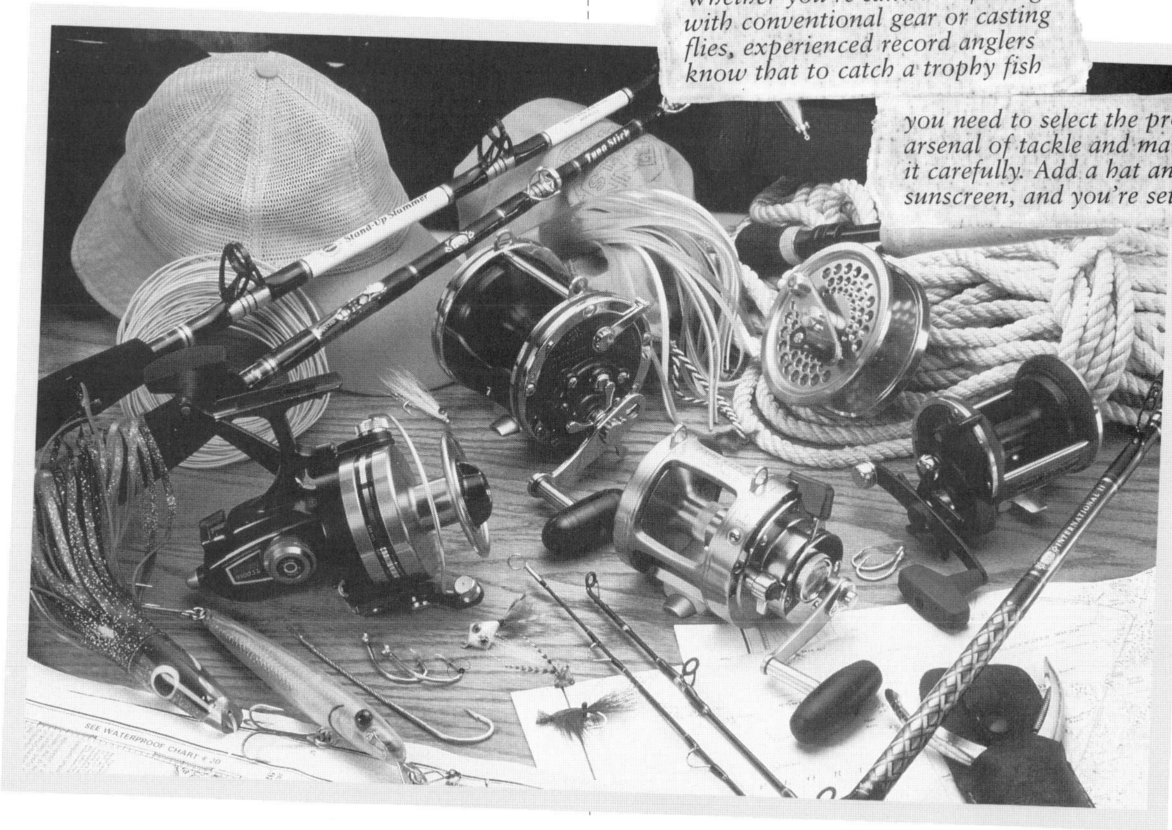

Whether you're saltwater fishing with conventional gear or casting flies, experienced record anglers know that to catch a trophy fish you need to select the proper arsenal of tackle and maintain it carefully. Add a hat and sunscreen, and you're set.

"Many anglers make the mistake of overwashing their reels. . . . I've even seen people dump their gear in the swimming pool, then lean it against the house to dry. Then they don't understand why the reel gets frozen up the next time they get a fish on. Reels can't absorb that much water. That's why it's important to first tighten the drag, then spray it off lightly with freshwater before drying."

—Tommy Green, custom tackle outfitter

and he trains his crew to walk an angler through the process of selecting gear. If a record-seeking angler enters looking for advice, Green will first determine what fish the angler is after and the line test he plans to fish. Since Green is familiar with current IGFA records—he once held his own record for snook—he'll counsel anglers if he thinks their goals are out of reach, suggesting another line class for a record that's more accessible. Then they'll talk specific tackle.

But in the long run, says Green, selecting the right tackle for your record-setting needs is a constant learning process. "I say to my customers, 'this year, after you've caught all your fish, come back here and tell me how good you are. Then next year, after you've learned a little more, tell me how dumb you were last year.' A true fisherman, if he keeps his mouth shut, listens, and observes, will learn more and be successful."

Quality Check

Early on in the process of selecting gear, you'll need to decide how much to spend on your rod and reel. (A simple spinning reel and rod can cost as little as $200, whereas a big-game boat rig for 130-pound [60 kg] test can cost a few thousand dollars. Custom-made gear can run much more.) On that point, Green tells the story of a guy whose goal was to spend lots of free time catching fish. For that reason, he built a new house on the water in southern Florida, then he bought a big sportfishing boat powered by twin diesel engines and tethered the glossy white vessel to his dock. Yet when it came to tackle, he decided to save some money and buy an economy rig. Then he complained that he couldn't catch any fish.

Cheaply made rods may lack the action and sensitivity that result in success on the fishing grounds. Choosing good quality gear can make or break a shot at a record fish. Yet experts say that many anglers don't know how to assess quality properly.

Some anglers recommend custom gear. "Any angler who is seriously pursuing records should have a custom rod made," says Farrier, who believes rods have come a long way since records were first pursued. Back in the 1940s, rods were 2 and 3 feet (0.6 to 0.9 m) longer than those used today, and the extra length put a lot more stress on the angler, rather than on the fish. "Reach and grip preferences are very personal. You need a rod that fits your own hand. I suggest testing several types. Pull on 'em in the shop and talk to a pro about having one of your own built. You may have a different opinion of what you need after you consult with an expert. The effort can save you a lot of grief and lost fish."

Whether you choose custom or production tackle, product knowledge is key. "The average angler isn't always aware of the subtle features that make for good quality fishing gear," says Green. For instance, it's important for a rod blank to have a straight spline. "One way to assess it is to bend the rod and study the guides. If the guides lean to the left or right as the blank is flexed, the spline isn't lined up. On the fishing grounds, that will decrease the pressure you can put on a fish." Green says it's also important to check the spacing of the guides on the rod. If you bend the rod and suddenly realize the line is dangerously rubbing against your hand or on the foregrip, there's a chance the first guide is positioned too far from the reel.

In addition to those tips, following are some general guidelines to consult when examining a saltwater rod or reel for purchase.

Rods

1. Sight along the length of the rod, checking for straightness as you rotate it.

2. Are the guides lined up straight and are the wrappings secure? Whatever the style of rod, the wraps need an even coat of varnish to prevent the wrapping thread from coming apart and fraying. Also note that guides come in two main styles. The single-foot variety is wrapped onto the blank by its sole projection. A two-foot version has twin projections so the guide is twice as secure. However, since the number of wraps on a guide are thought to affect a rod's action, many anglers prefer the single-foot version, which requires half as many wraps.

3. If the handle is made of cork, is it solid and snug? Avoid cork that's dried and cracked, with lots of pits and gouges.

4. Is the reel seat snug and secure? The best way to tell is to try it, either with a borrowed reel or one you bring to the tackle shop with you.

5. How does the rod feel? You can cast a half-dozen rods of the same length, weight, and material but made by different manufacturers, and you might have six different reactions. The only infallible method of determining how well you like a rod is to conduct a hands-on trial. A good tackle shop will allow you to rig a candidate with reel and line, then take it outside and cast until you get a good feeling for the rod's particular properties and idiosyncrasies.

Reels

1. Brass or steel are extremely durable materials for reels. So are such man-made materials as graphite.

2. Look and feel for any imperfections. Check the finish. Reels with thick coats of finish are

more scratch-resistant than those with thin anodized or baked finishes. Also, reel feet that are screwed on are stronger than ones that are riveted.

3 Check for loose, wobbling parts as you wind the reel, especially the spool and the spool release.

4 Make sure the spool is large enough to accommodate enough line for the type of fishing you plan to do. That's a particularly important consideration in bluewater ocean fishing, since there's always the possibility of hooking a big fish that takes long runs. Choose a reel with at least 200 yards (180 m) of line capacity.

Care and Maintenance

Caring for and maintaining gear properly has always been a crucial key to success in fishing. Even in the 1930s, when line made from linen was reeling in trophy fish, anglers had to remove the line—which was prone to rot—from the spool after each fishing excursion and rinse it with freshwater before laying it to dry on a special rack. Maintaining tackle and terminal tackle is still time-consuming, but doing it properly will increase your success. "I once watched Kelly Everett [who has the men's 30-pound line test record for blue marlin] sit at his kitchen table for 30 minutes sharpening one hook, taking pains not to overheat the metal," says Green. "That's the kind of meticulous preparation it takes to be good."

Human negligence is the greatest enemy of fishing gear. Following are some things to keep in mind when caring for your saltwater tackle.

Rods

1 To extend the life of your saltwater rod, clean it thoroughly after each use. Fleece mitts, the kind used to wash car bodies, make good tackle cleaners. Dip one into soapy water and swab the rod, then rinse the rod in freshwater to remove all traces of corrosive salt. Use a soft brush to remove dried fish scales or dried algae.

2 Dry the rod with a clean, soft cloth or chamois, paying attention to the ferrules, guides, and reel seat. If any of these components are bent, the rod's action will be affected. You don't want to discover that a component needs repair after a record fish is on your line.

3 To store your rod, put it in a cloth sleeve to keep dust and other dirt off. When transporting your rod, place it in a hard protective case. This will greatly reduce the chance of it's being damaged. Many anglers know of at least one person who broke an unprotected rod by slamming a car door on it.

Reels

1 If you drop a reel, immediately clean off any dirt, sand, or other debris that may have gotten into the mechanism. Also, make sure that no screws have come loose. If it's a spinning reel, check to see that the pick-up bail is not bent.

2 Saltwater reels should be lightly rinsed in freshwater after each use to remove any traces of salt. If possible, remove the spool to allow any water trapped there to evaporate. "Many anglers make the mistake of overwashing their reels," says Green. "I've even seen people dump their gear in the swimming pool, then lean it against the house to dry. Then they don't understand why the reel gets frozen up the next time they get a fish on. Reels can't absorb that much water. That's why it's important to first tighten the drag, then spray it off lightly with freshwater before drying."

Dry the reel with a clean absorbent cloth, then lightly oil the internal moving parts with reel oil. After reassembling the reel, put just a drop of household oil on any external moving parts.

3 Any drag mechanism that includes cork or rubber should be kept fully released when the reel is not in use. Otherwise, the soft material will become indented, stiff, or both.

4 Before storing your reel, let it dry in open air. But bear in mind that the need to store and transport reels in cases is as important as it is for rods. Leather or cloth reel bags are designed for that purpose. Padded reel cases are even sturdier. So are tackle boxes in which many anglers keep their bait-casting and spinning reels safe and secure amid plugs, hooks, and other gear.

General Considerations When Selecting Saltwater Tackle

The type of saltwater rod and reel you select for your record fishing pursuit will depend on the species and size of fish you're after. To help you make an informed choice, following is some general information on the most popular types of saltwater gear.

1 Spinning tackle. Introduced before World War II, spinning tackle has long been the most popular form of saltwater gear, although recent improvements in other types of tackle have attracted the attentions of both inshore and offshore anglers. The reason for its surge to success was its ability to cast very light lures or baits with no risk of backlash. (A backlash occurs only on a conventional spool reel, which revolves. When the spool is turning faster than the line coming off the reel, line billows up on the reel into a tangle.) This is possible because there is no rotating spool, which needs relatively heavy bait to activate it. Instead, line is pulled off a revolving spool by a fish running against the drag, and replaced on a stationary spool when the handle is cranked and line is regained.

Spinning gear has one drawback: line twist, which occurs when you turn the handle while the line is going out. Twist worsens when line isn't placed back on the spool. Line twist can be deadly for a record fisherman because it weakens the line significantly if

Reel History

IF THERE'S ONE name in tackle that's often associated with world record fish, it's Penn. This Pennsylvania-based tackle company was founded just six years after the IGFA was established. The two organizations grew up together, and since Penn became one of the largest manufacturers of fishing tackle in this country, there were more of its reels on the fishing grounds than any other.

Penn reels, in particular, have been on the pulling end of many fantastic fish, but perhaps the most famous is the all-tackle record for white shark. In 1959, Alfred Dean of Australia caught a 2,664-pound (1,208.38 kg) shark with a Penn offshore reel spooled with 130-pound (60 kg) line. It took him about an hour to land the fish, but even more impressive is the fact that Dean caught this man-eating great white while fishing from the beach in Ceduna, South Australia.

Dean's catch silenced the cynics who contended that records were only for wealthy anglers with the financial resources to travel the world, charter yachts with professional crews, and fish with custom-made equipment. Dean was a local who had been fishing the area for almost 20 years. Not all of his fishing was from shore, though. To get shots at the massive whites that prowled the surrounding water for seals, Dean would fish from small boats owned by local commercial fishermen. He would pack his own equipment for these adventures, including a fighting chair he had

(continued on next page)

Penn Reels have been on the pulling end of many fantastic fish, but the most famous is Alfred Dean's 2,644-pound (1,208.38 kg) white shark, the largest fish ever landed on rod and reel. It was caught in 1959 while Dean fished from shore with a Penn 14/0 spooled with 130-pound (60 kg) line.

Reel History

continued from page 90

made from an old tractor seat, which he would bolt to a stern platform.

Dean was a grape grower by profession, a man who worked the vineyards he'd inherited from his deceased father. "When a crop came in I put away enough for another fishing trip," he told David Potts and Dale Shaw of *TRUE* magazine (April 1959). "When that trip was over I started saving for another. The weight of my catches went up steadily as I learned the waters and the ways of sharks. I hit 1,000 pounds (453 kg), then 1,200 (544 kg). But I saw sharks so big I shook looking at them. I'd throw them a bait and some little bastard would shoot in and take it out of the big one's jaws. But every time I'd miss a big one I'd learn something."

It seems Dean taught himself well. Almost 40 years later, his white shark stands as the largest fish ever caught on rod and reel according to IGFA rules.

there is a strong pull on it at the time the twisting occurs. Monofilament line typically stretches from 30 to 40 percent under heavy load; if it's twisted simultaneously, as much as 30 percent of its strength can be lost. That's why an angler fighting an exceptionally big fish for a long period of time is facing steadily increasing odds that the outcome will favor the fish.

Of course, there are many anglers who are proficient with this type of gear. In fact, Green says some of his customers catch swordfish and blue marlin on spinning tackle. But when it comes to large fish, Green says his customers catch more world records on conventional (bait-casting) tackle.

Today's spinning gear uses monofilament lines from 2- to 30-pound (1 to 15 kg) test. However, some experts contend that anything over 20-pound (10 kg) test casts poorly. As for features, the most popular type of retrieve mechanism is the bail, a metal hoop across the face of the spool. Open the bail manually with your finger; it closes with a crank of the handle. Drag is adjusted by tightening or loosening a nut located at the front of the spool or at the rear. Regardless of the features you select, the choice of spinning reel should be based on line weight and line capacity. For instance, a medium spinner is designed for 16- to 30-pound (8 to 15 kg) test; a light rig is for 8- to 16-pound (4 to 8 kg) test.

When you're selecting a spinning rod, important factors to consider are length and stiffness. The best spinning materials are graphite or graphite-fiberglass composites. Fiberglass rods are still used, but their action is softer and they are heavier.

2 Bait-casting tackle. Many experts say that of all the forms of light tackle (excluding stand-up rigs) bait-casting gear is the most efficient for fighting a big fish, followed by fly tackle and then spinning. With bait-casting tackle, there is no problem with reel-induced line twist. That's because the line is cast and retrieved by a revolving spool. Backlashing used to be a problem with these reels, but mechanical developments have changed that. In the 1940s, anglers relied on an educated thumb to prevent a birds nest formed by fishing line. Then came the inertial braking system of the 1950s, and then the magnetic casting brakes of the 1970s and 1980s, which limit the speed at which the spool revolves during a cast. Today, reels with the latest magnetic brake systems and semi-stationary line-guard designs work well with very light lines.

Bait-casting tackle is an effective fish-fighting tool for the way it can apply drag. You can use your left thumb to apply additional pressure while the right hand continues to crank the handle. Unlike spinning tackle, this gear requires no hand-shifting.

Two types of drag systems are available. The star drag consists of a series of disks that increase or decrease pressure against the spool's drum. It's a durable system operated by one or two star-shaped wheels mounted between the reel casing and the winder. The lever drag system contains a single lever attached to one large disk that exerts pressure against the reel drum. Many record fishermen prefer bait-casting reels with this system, since it's very sensitive and often easier to use.

Bait-casting reels for blue water are typically made of anodized aluminum or graphite to resist corrosion. When selecting a matching rod, follow the same guidelines as you would for spinning tackle: think stiffness and durable materials. However, guide placement is more critical on a bait-casting rig.

Of all the forms of light tackle, many experts say bait-casting gear is the most efficient for fighting a big fish, followed by fly tackle and then spinning. With bait-casting tackle, there is no problem with reel-induced line twist. One of the popular reels for boats is the Shimano TLD-20.

3 Big-game tackle. The biggest improvements since the 1940s in this gear, which today can handle a line as light as 20 pounds (10 kg), have been in rods. In the old days, tips were made of laminated strips of wood or bamboo, and rated by their various weights in ounces. Today, they are made of fiberglass, graphite, or a composite of the two. A rating by tip weight would be meaningless. Instead, they are classed by the lines they are designed to be used with.

Big-game tackle is designed not for casting but for trolling or still fishing with live bait. The rod guides most preferred by record fishermen are the roller type, which reduce friction and protect the line, particularly during long fights. However, these guides also require more maintenance than the fixed-ring type; lubricate regularly.

A popular material for big-game rod butts of all line classes is machined and anodized marine grade aluminum.

As for reels, choose one with the appropriate capacity and quality. The pricier custom, collectible models available can cost as much as some automobiles, but the less expensive reels in the top-of-the-line category, such as Fin-Nor, Penn, the Shimano Beastmaster, or Daiwa Sealine Tournament, are very capable.

4 Stand-up tackle. In recent years, more big-game anglers have given up the fighting chair and conventional tackle for stand-up gear and are setting records in the process. In fact, many anglers who are familiar with both conventional and stand-up tackle contend that the same line test can be used more effectively on this relatively new type of gear.

Stand-up fishing rods and related equipment evolved aboard southern California long-range party boats during the late 1970s, where anglers wielding conventional rigs were getting whipped at the rails by yellowfin tuna and marlin. Gradually, these anglers started experimenting with shorter and shorter rods, and as a result the number of successful big-fish landings increased.

Compared with the standard 7-foot (2.3 m) big-game rod for a fighting chair rod, the average stand-up rod is 5½ to 6 feet (1.68 to 1.83 m) long. (If you're under 6 feet tall, experts suggest you have a custom rod built that's no longer than your height.) These short, powerful rods have roller guides, a long foregrip (at least 16 inches [40 cm] is recommended) and a low reel position that gives the angler more leverage over the fish.

"I change my line constantly. Remember, line can stretch, take abrasions, and dry out after you fight a single fish."

—Captain Bob Rocchetta,
Orient Point, New York

When selecting a reel for big-game record fishing, it's important to choose one with the appropriate capacity and quality. The pricier custom models available can cost thousands of dollars, but the less expensive reels in the top-of-the-line category, such as models from Fin-Nor, Shimano, Daiwa, and Penn, are very capable. The Penn 50 SW International is pictured here in close-up (above) and in use (left).

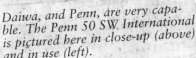

Fighting a fish with conventional tackle in a fighting chair requires the angler either to pull with the back muscles or push with the legs, depending on the type of harness used. With stand-up tackle, the work is done with the leg and pelvic muscles. Using short, quick, pumping strokes, it's possible for the angler to bring a fish to the boat in less time.

The most popular range of stand-up tackle seems to be 20- to 80-pound (10 to 37 kg) test, with 50-pound-class (24 kg) gear rated as very capable of landing most species that can be caught with this tackle. Custom builders can tailor a specialized rod to your specifications, but there are a lot of good off-the shelf sticks, too, including models from Daiwa, Penn, and Shimano. An additional advantage of using a stand-up rod is that you can pair it with a conventional reel.

Good-quality, well-balanced tackle is a crucial component for any record-setting strategy. It can't guarantee success, particularly since history shows some prize-winning fish have been caught on marginal rigs, including reels with drags gone jerky with corrosion and hooks turned dull from neglect. However, tackle chosen carefully and kept in top condition can only increase your odds of winning a long and fair battle.

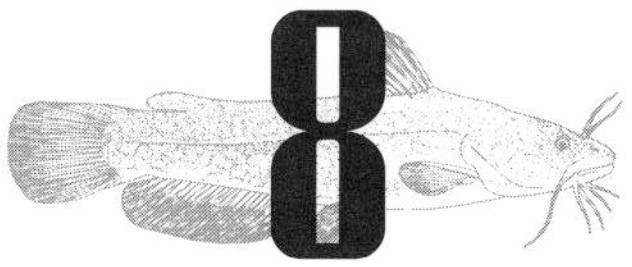

8

How to Target Records

Secrets from the Pros

Throughout this book, there has been a lot said about targeting records. All kinds of people target trophy fish. In addition to the anglers who do so seeking new challenges and fishing fame, many professional captains devote their considerable experience and knowledge to the pursuit of records. Some captains do so for the thrill of competition; others hunt the giants of a species to better their careers in the business of sportfishing. Regardless of the motivation, those who are successful record hunters have a keen notion of what's required to target an unforgettable fish properly.

To help you understand what is involved in the process of targeting records, I've asked some well-known captains and anglers to describe how they would go about targeting a species of their choice. Following are their theories. Although you may not be planning to pursue any of the fish listed here, at the very least you'll come away with a good sense of what's required to prepare a record-setting strategy properly. As you'll see, the right approach to this challenge requires thorough research, flexibility, some radical thinking, and a little help from the fish.

King Mackerel

R. T. Trosset of Key West, Florida, is one of record fishing's most famous captains, with well over 100 IGFA marks to his credit. His achievements are considerable, yet this guide of 23 years readily acknowledges that many exceptional records have been landed not because of the angler's prowess, but due to the fact that the fish decided to cooperate. He recalls the day angler Jeanne Duval caught a 54-pound, 8-ounce (24.72 kg) king mackerel on 12-pound (6 kg) line. "We fought it for close to an hour, but it wasn't until a porpoise

> *"Targeting records is a team sport. . . . You can't be with people who turn their backs on you and keep fishing while you're battling a potential record. They have to be on the same wavelength as you, especially when the fish comes to the surface."*
>
> —Terry Rudnik, author and halibut expert

"Fish are basically lazy, and they won't go out of their way to get food if they can have something else for free."

—Peter Frederiksen, author and former charter captain

came into the area that things started looking up for us. I believe the kingfish got scared, and in a panic, swam up against the boat for protection. Thanks to the porpoise, our record fish made a crucial mistake."

King mackerel—or kingfish—are a favorite species of Trosset, who operates the 28-foot (8.5 m) center console *Spindrift* out of Oceanside Marina. This captain says his goal is to get to 200 records, which he thinks will take about two more years. And if he were targeting trophy king mackerel—which some call *smokers*—he would choose to fish with a woman, because of the number of open records for women, and with 8-pound (4 kg) test line. The existing record is 41 pounds (18.59 kg), but Trosset fishes waters where an average kingfish is 40 pounds (18 kg). Use big baits, however, and you could see 60- to 70-pounders (27.21 to 31.75 kg) behind the boat, although that would be a very good day. (The all-tackle king mackerel record of 90 pounds [40.82 kg] was caught from Key West in 1976.)

"Eight-pound [4 kg] test is a reasonable line for anglers with some light-line experience," says Trosset, although he likes to start his clients with 20-pound (10 kg) test to assess their skill level. "Going under 8-pound requires a lot more skill, from both the angler and crew."

As for timing, Trosset advises planning a few two-day trips to Key West over the course of three months: December to February, when kingfish are in the area. Where you fish will depend on conditions and the time of year; typically, kingfish are on the Atlantic side in January and in the Gulf come February.

To catch big fish, big live baits are required. For instance, Trosset sometimes fishes in gear pulling a 1-pound (0.45 kg) blue runner, which is large enough to keep the 30-pound (13.6 kg) kingfish away. Baits are rigged on spinning tackle, which he recommends for its fast retrieve abilities. "Eighty percent of my clients do great with this tackle. I don't want them to have to worry about putting the line back on the reel."

Fair warning: You'll pull a lot of hooks on kingfish. "When a hook gets moved back and forth in this fish's mouth, it has a tendency to slide out," says Trosset. "It can be heartbreaking. To avoid that problem, try not to pull the fish directly toward you. Instead, fight the fish with the hook always lodged at the corner of the king mackerel's mouth, even if that means you have to climb all over the boat to follow the fish."

When working with advanced anglers, Trosset often recommends employing the drop-back technique for this species. Often

"If you're just standing there with an 8-pound line-class rig waiting for something to happen, it probably won't. You have to get the action going. Remember, the more fish you catch, the more will show up."

—R. T. Trosset, 100+ records

a kingfish will slice through half of your bait on the first bite, devouring the rear portion. (That's why many experienced charter skippers rig a second hook farther back in the bait, often hidden just under the skin.) "When that happens, I tell anglers to open the bail, drop to free spool, and let the other half of the bait sink. Chances are good another fish will come up for it. In fact, hookups are more common on that second bite."

Although Trosset is an expert at targeting record fish on specific line classes, his experience has taught him that, to be successful in this game, you have to be flexible and come prepared to catch more than just the species you're after. "If you're just standing there with an 8-pound [4 kg] line-class rig waiting for something to happen, it probably won't. You have to get the action going. Remember, the more fish you catch, the more will show up."

Pacific Halibut

Some record fish require more than skill and commitment from ambitious anglers. Pacific halibut will demand that you spend some of your hard-earned cash, since the trophy-sized specimens are accessible for recreational anglers only in places that are far off the beaten track.

Terry Rudnik, a resident of Olympia, Washington, and author of *How to Catch Trophy Halibut*, assures us that the current line-class records for this huge bottom feeder of the Pacific coast are very impressive. To beat the existing marks, you might well need to make a trip to an outpost of Alaska. The Aleutian Islands of southwestern Alaska, which extend in an arc 1,200 miles (1,900 km) from the Alaskan peninsula, are accessible only by jet from Anchorage, yet here big Pacific halibut (those over 160 pounds [72 kg]) are abundant. Specifically, you want to head to Dutch Harbor, where there are favorable fishing conditions and minimal competition from other recreational anglers.

Dutch Harbor, which is near the town of Unalaska, offers calm, protected water where you can fish for these deep-swimmers in water as shallow as 200 feet (60 m). There's ample food for them to feed on, herring, for instance, and just as important, there are only three to four dozen anglers fishing on any given day. Those low numbers are advantageous to record seekers, particularly since halibut are becoming a more popular gamefish for recreational anglers due to the decline in salmon stocks.

The best time to target your record, says Rudnik, is between May and October. As for reasonable records to target, Rudnik would shoot for the men's 12- or 16-pound (6 or 8 kg) line class since those marks are near 170 pounds (77.11 kg). For women, there are reasonable marks under 170 at 20-pound (10 kg) line and under.

If there's one crew that's operating on good momentum, it's the team aboard *Suzanne Marie*, a boat owned by John Lucking, which has taken the last two all-tackle records for Pacific halibut. Like many other charter boats, *Suzanne Marie* doesn't mess with baits; lead heads and big white plastic grubs are eye candy for big flatties.

A more important consideration when targeting record halibut is to choose your crew carefully. "It's a team sport," says Rudnik. "You can't be with people who turn their backs on you and keep fishing while you're battling a potential record. They have to be on the same wavelength as you, especially when the fish comes to the surface.

You'll probably have one chance at a halibut. They don't lay there and let you poke 'em with a gaff. They'll head for the bottom, and it's rare to see a halibut a second time."

A good crew comes prepared. They are familiar with the rules for landing this massive fish and have the right equipment to do so. Although a Pacific halibut may appear to have quit fighting, it may not be dead: it can still thrash around dangerously and because of its great size should always be handled very carefully.

Spanish Mackerel

The IGFA all-tackle record, made in North Carolina in 1987, is 13 pounds (5.89 kg) for Spanish mackerel, but it has been caught commercially to almost 20 pounds (10 kg). Since many of the line-class records are under 10 pounds (4.5 kg), it is certainly feasible to have a shot at beating some of the existing marks. The range of this excellent gamefish is the greatest of all Atlantic mackerels, from Brazil north to New Jersey, and occasionally as far up as Cape Cod, so it is accessible to anglers in a variety of locales. And because this coastal fish will wander into inlets and bays, it's available to small-boat anglers, pier and bridge fishermen, and sometimes surfcasters. But a particularly good choice is the west coast of Florida.

Captain James Wisner, 45, has been fishing Tampa Bay waters for seven years, during which time he's scored 10 records for himself and another 17 for family and friends from his 23-foot (7 m) Dorado center console, *Wiz*. Although he contends that every record in the IGFA book is breakable, Wisner is also wisely cautious about suggesting where, when, and how an angler should fish for records.

"The only consistency in fishing is inconsistency. No one can say trophy fish will be at a certain place at a certain time. It's too unpredictable, which is why you can't always plan a record-fishing attempt around a one-week vacation. You need to be flexible, and you need a pinch of luck. However, I will say that I fish in one of the best areas for Spanish mackerel."

Tampa Bay is the second largest estuary in the United States. It has many of the qualities that attract big fish, including plenty of baitfish. To catch a trophy-sized Spanish mackerel, Wisner suggests wetting a line in the fall, when bigger fish come close in to feed on the baitfish that are starting to swim offshore. Ideal water temperatures are between 71° and 76°F (21° to 24°C).

Wisner is most successful fishing live baits—sardines, cigar minnows, and threadfin herring are three good choices—in a chum slick. As for special considerations, he says "You need a lot of bait for this type of record fishing, and a good aerated livewell onboard that can hold over 300 sardines. When you get a fish up in the slick, you want to have plenty of live bait available to throw out."

As in real estate, location is key for record fishing. Wisner suggests spending time in shallow water along the edges of grass flats, where big Spanish mackerel roam in search of bait schools that are preparing to depart for deeper water. He's also had exceptional success along the shoulders of the shipping channel. There, among rock piles that rise as high as 15 feet (5 m) from the bottom, he's caught 16 of his record fish. "Bait piles up there," he says. "And you can locate the structure with a good depthfinder."

Light tackle is recommended for this species; however, Wisner asks his clients to assess their skills honestly before fishing some of the ultralight lines. "Many people think they are better anglers than they really are," he says. "They don't realize you need a very light touch to be successful with line between 2 and 8 pounds [1 and 4 kg]. Some people forget that skill level determines record-fishing success. If you don't have the right technique for light line, a record fishing attempt will be very frustrating."

Captain Bob Rocchetta, who took the men's 50-pound (24 kg) line-class record for striped bass with a 76-pounder (34.47 kg), says there could be a future record swimming out near Montauk, New York. (Courtesy Bob Rocchetta)

Striped Bass

Captain Bob Rocchetta remembers the night he caught the 76-pound (34.47 kg) striped bass that stands as a men's 50-pound (24 kg) line-class record, and is the former all-tackle mark for the species. On July 17, 1981, he was fishing from his boat off Montauk Point, New York, during a fantastic, full eclipse of the moon. "The eclipse ended at about 4:30 A.M. That's when I caught the fish. It was such a beautiful thing. Like a special gift from the lunar spirits."

Divine intervention isn't necessary to catch a record striper today, but a little help from above couldn't hurt, since this species is one of the most sought after in salt water. Striper addicts take their fishing seriously. They're willing to trudge miles along jagged shorelines to reach booming surf where stripers have been rumored to gather. They creep and crawl over barnacle-encrusted rocks and fish late into the night. Others battle sleepiness and fatigue from the wet decks of boats rocking in the sea. Sure, other fish grow bigger and fight harder, and one or two may taste better, but this is one of very few species that rates high in all of those categories.

The striped bass can grow to exceed 80 pounds (36 kg), and there have been reports of commercially netted stripers that have weighed over 100 pounds (45 kg), but any striped bass over 50 pounds (22.5 kg) is certainly worth bragging about, and the average today is closer to 10 or 20 pounds (4.5 to 9 kg). However, 18 of the 20 existing line-class records are well over 30 pounds (13.5 kg), with the all-tackle mark at 78 pounds, 8 ounces (35.60 kg, New Jersey, 1982). Where, then, can you find monster stripers to rival the existing records?

Montauk Point at the eastern tip of Long Island is one of the greatest striped bass fishing areas in the world. Here it's possible to catch them by surf-casting or from one of the charter boats specially designed for use close to the wild and rocky surf. The biggest bulls arrive here late in May and

Choosing a Charter Guide

IN MANY CASES, an angler's ability to capture a world record successfully depends on the talents of hired hands, namely charter guides, captains, or crews. Selecting the right expert for your record-fishing goals is no big mystery, but it does require some work.

Most anglers begin their search for a reputable guide by consulting a travel agent who specializes in fishing expeditions. A good agent will interview you about your angling goals and then recommend the appropriate boat and crew for your needs. The advantage of working with a travel agent is that this professional has a wealth of information at his or her fingertips. However, that shouldn't stop you from doing additional research.

Some anglers also consult magazines for leads on well-known captains and crews. Others call the International Game Fish Association for recommendations. For instance, if you are planning to target a record in the Florida Keys, you can ask the IGFA for the number of a representative in that area. The IGFA rep may have substantial knowledge of local charter operations.

Once you have the name of a guide or crew, take the time to collect references (three to five anglers who have fished on the boat) and then *contact them*. "Word of mouth referrals are key in this business," says Mike Fitzgerald, co-owner of Frontiers International Travel in Pennsylvania. Questions to ask your references include

- Is the captain/crew knowledgeable about IGFA rules?
- Can they rig lines and leaders to IGFA specifications?
- Do they know how to weigh a record and where to go to do it?

It's important that the captain/crew you choose understands how important the record hunt is to you. I heard a story recently about a man who caught a trophy trevally at Christmas Island. The captain knew his client was after an IGFA listing, but apparently it wasn't much of a priority for this hired hand. When the boat had docked, the captain got busy with chores and the angler ran off to tell a friend about his special catch. Neither man was watching when a local picked up the trevally and walked it over to a cleaning station, where she proceeded to gut the fish.

When talking with references, ask about the type of gear provided on the charter boat. You want to fish with quality equipment in good condition, particularly when it comes to reels. For that information, you must rely on references. If you plan on traveling with your own fishing gear, find out if the captain can inspect your equipment to make sure it complies with IGFA regulations.

Fitzgerald also recommends interviewing the captain or crew before deciding to schedule a trip. However, it's not always necessary to ask if the captain or crew has set records in the past. "More important," says Fitzgerald, "is to determine if they have experience fishing for world records. Remember, a crew can know all the rules and possess excellent technique but lose records due to the angler's shortcomings."

Ideally, you want to choose a charter professional with a proven track record. If the professional has no records, you can check that person's reputation in other *(continued on next page)*

Choosing a Charter Guide

continued from page 100

ways. For instance, in well-known fishing ports such as Cabo San Lucas or Kona, huge tournaments are organized on a regular basis. You can review the tournament records of a crew you're interested in; find out how well they fished and if they placed.

As for the cost of a charter, that depends on where you're fishing and on the experience of the captain/crew.

"Anywhere there's a great fishing resource, you'll find more than one charter boat operating in that area," says Fitzgerald. "Call around to get an average cost. Keep in mind, however, that the hot captains with good tournament standings and a few records to their credit can charge top dollar. It's up to you to decide whether you think the experience is worth the extra $200 to $400 per day."

remain until the middle of December, but Rocchetta says a record-hunter should get most of his or her fishing in between July and October. (All four current records over 70 pounds [31.75 kg] were caught in the New York–New Jersey area between May and October of their respective years.)

Many anglers find that surf-casting from the wild and wind-whipped shore is the more exciting and adventurous way to hunt for this species, but the truth is that boat fishing is more efficient in record-fishing terms. On a boat, you're not limited by how far you can cast, plus you have the option to bottom fish, drift, or troll. Rocchetta, 50, who now guides out of Orient Point on the north side of Long Island, fishes from a 25-foot (11.25 kg) Parker, *Northern Lights*.

Like so many experienced charter captains in the area, he looks for these fish past tide rips, where the current clashes with underwater boulders, around rocks, and near wrecks and piers, although shellfish beds have proven to be exceptionally good striper grounds. He also thinks you can find stripers near kelp beds. "I think they like to get down in them because crabs are there. They'll feed on crabs when there aren't fish around. I know this because I've boated stripers with kelp lice on them."

It's fortunate for anglers that striped bass will eat almost anything, including less appetizing items such as cigarette lighters. However, serious anglers have success with lures and natural baits. Many feel if the striper is feeding, a live bait is the best ammunition. However, an artificial lure could pique the striper's curiosity, too. Rocchetta's experience near Montauk has taught him to use fresh-cut bunker during summer days and eels at night. In the fall, he goes to eels. Typically, he'll drift the boat over structure and drop the bait with a bottom-fishing rig.

"You can catch this fish on almost anything," he says. "But for record fishing, the trick is to have your tackle ready. I've seen many people hook potential records and never land them because their tackle wasn't up to snuff. Either the drag is sticky or the knots are wrong. Line is a problem, too. This fish can break 50-pound [24 kg] test like it was sewing thread. That's why I change my line constantly. Remember, line can stretch, take abrasions, and dry out after you fight a single fish."

Although Rocchetta can't guarantee that the Montauk area will yield a bull striper, with proper preparation, you can increase your odds of taking a trophy. "I can give you the basic elements and information. God gives you the rest. Records are a gift, and the day you catch one will be a special day indeed."

Black Drum

For some people, record fishing is a cakewalk. Take Captain Joe Porcelli, for instance. This resident of Lake Helen, Florida, has guided anglers to eight world records, six of which have been for black drum. "I spend all of my summer days sight-casting to snook, tarpon, redfish, and trout. Push poling the flats in my 18-footer [6 m] is hard work. That's why I look forward to black drum season. It's easy by comparison."

Porcelli made news in 1998 when he and angler Raleigh Werking broke the existing 4-pound (2 kg) line-class record with a whopping 90-pound, 8-ounce (41.04 kg) fish. That catch was the fourth record he and Werking caught as a team, yet Porcelli believes there's potential to break more on this species. "Three of those records could be in the women's line-class category; that is, if I can get my wife Jennifer out there," says Porcelli. Which are doable for tenacious anglers? For women, all except the 50- and 80-pound (24 and 37

Captain Joe Porcelli prides himself on his abilities to find trophy-sized black drum and to release them, too.

Here, he revives a 90-pound (40.5 kg) drum that recently set a record for Raleigh Werking. (Courtesy Joe Porcelli)

kg) line-class records, which are fish 93 pounds (42.18 kg) and up. For men, perhaps the 4-pound (2 kg) record, now at 56 pounds (25.40 kg), and maybe even the 8-pound (4 kg) line-class record, which is 82 pounds, 8 ounces (37.42 kg).

To target these records, says Porcelli, a good plan is to fish in his stomping grounds: the North Indian River at Ponce Inlet between Daytona and New Smyrna, Florida. That advice will surprise anglers familiar with the records. After all, the largest fish—those over 100 pounds (45 kg)—have consistently come from the Virginia-Maryland-Delaware area. Yet Porcelli contends his local waters produce trophy fish, too. And he's invested years of trial-and-error fishing learning the habits of the big fish.

"Most of the fish we catch here are in the 50- to 65-pound [22.5 to 29.25 kg] range, but at the right time of year, for every 10 fish we get there's a 70- or 80-pounder [31.5 or 36 kg]."

The best time of year for record seekers is mating season, when black drum migrate through the channel out to the surf to lay eggs. Porcelli likes to catch the fish as they return from spawning. That way, he doesn't disrupt reproduction. In addition, the fish are easier to catch. "They're full of piss and vinegar on the way out. But when they return, they're tired."

Although February to April are good months for black drum, Porcelli knows when mating season has arrived: that's when male black drum will use their air bladders to create sounds similar to drums beating. The theory is that the sound helps the fish locate and attract female drums. "I hear them coming as they migrate toward us from Titusville to the south. I usually hear them singing when they reach Haulover Channel. At that point, I know they'll be thick in our area within a few weeks."

Porcelli recommends fishing for black drum at night, since they don't feed as well when there's a lot of noise (from boat traffic, etc.). He double-anchors his 18-foot (5.5 m) Archercraft in anywhere from 4 to 15 feet (1 to 4.5 m) of water and puts out four conventional rigs, each baited with blue crabs that are fished on the bottom. The tricky part is "detecting the strike," says Porcelli. "These fish eat so light, they barely put weight on the rod. A brim in a pond can bend the rod more. Black drum find the food with their barbels and gently pick it up with their big lips. I'd say 99 percent of the bites are very subtle. On top of that, they're slow and docile. No greyhounding." Although sluggish on the strike, once hooked, black drum put up a good fight, although some have called it uninspired. It rarely makes runs of even medium length. For this reason, sporting anglers prefer light over heavy tackle, and landing this fish on light gear is primarily a matter of patience.

As for special considerations, this captain—who has over 20 years experience on charter boats—encourages catch and release. In fact, Porcelli released Werking's 90-pound (40.5 kg) fish last year. "We keep

> *"The hot captains with good tournament standings and a few records to their credit can charge top dollar. It's up to you to decide whether you think the experience is worth the extra $200 to $400 per day."*
>
> —Mike Fitzgerald

> *"My advice for a record seeker is don't be afraid to lose fish. The more pressure you put on them, the better your chances of landing a record. Know the maximum limits of your drag."*
>
> —Captain Troy Perez

a scale onboard, along with cameras and measuring tapes. After the catch, I'll run in to shore, beach the boat, weigh the fish, and then let it go."

Bluefish

A logical strategy is important if you want to be successful at the record-fishing game, but there's a lot to be said for taking chances, too. Consider bluefish, for instance. More than half the current line-class records were taken off North Carolina, the same state to produce the all-tackle bluefish of 31 pounds, 12 ounces (14.40 kg) in 1972. But just because that state has an excellent track record doesn't mean you have to be there to win. If you're equipped with local knowledge of other prolific bluefish grounds, you're in the running for a record.

Peter Frederiksen, author of *How To Catch Bluefish* and a senior editor at *Yachting* magazine, contends that anglers with a working knowledge of the New York Bight stand a reasonable chance of taking a record, particularly those anglers with good light-tackle and fly-fishing skills.

Bluefish range worldwide and are found in all major temperate seas except for possibly the North Pacific, yet most of us think of this hard-striking, ferociously hungry fish as the darling of the East Coast of North America. In the New York Bight—that L-shaped area that encompasses the south shore of Long Island and extends south and west to the coast of New Jersey—anglers crowd aboard private boats and a slew of party boats to try their luck with this toothy species. They fish day and night, employing all types of tackle and techniques. With so many on the water, competition could be heady, but Frederiksen believes that the head count is high here because there are so many fish. And in the world of record fishing, getting a lot of shots at your target species is the name of the game.

Here, the average size of a fat fish is 20 pounds (9 kg); good news, since most of the standing line-class records are under 26 pounds (11.7 kg), with one light-line record under 15 pounds (6.75 kg). Bluefish season extends from May through November or December, but Frederiksen says there's often a lull in action some time in July, when the fish move off to spawn. In May, newly arrived bluefish are called *racers* because of their big heads and skinny bodies. But once they've settled in for the summer at the New York Bight, dining on baitfish as well as the abundant chum slicks produced by local boats all day and all night, these sport fish get big.

Chumming is the most popular way to draw these sometimes finicky feeders to your boat, and it's the recommended technique for light-tackle and fly-fishing gear. Chum is made from ground menhaden (bunker) and should be watered down with seawater to disperse more readily. Also, it helps to toss a few chunks of cut butterfish or smelts into the slick to "sweeten" it from time to time. There are other ways to increase the efficiency of a chum slick. "Don't overdo it," says Frederiksen. "Otherwise you'll overfeed the fish and they won't come after your bait." Frederiksen also advises anglers to make sure they're fishing baits where the chum is. "If the tide is really ripping, I'll put chum out from the side of the boat instead of the back. That way, it sinks as it passes under the boat, and the line remains in the slick, where it should be. Fish are basically lazy, and they won't go out of their way to get food if they can have something else for free."

The rigging needed to fish for big blues with light tackle isn't complicated, but it does require some sort of shock leader to protect the line from those extremely sharp teeth. I suggest rigging up at least 100 5/0 reverse-bend bronze hooks with short #7, #8, or #9 wire leaders. If the fish blitz, you will go through them in a hurry and you don't want to use the same rig twice. If the bait goes deep into the fish's throat, the bluefish will chew on it and the leader will kink or bend, which can weaken it. Use dark stainless-steel wire and a small black barrel swivel between the wire leader and main line. Three to 4 inches of wire is sufficient; use a haywire twist to connect the hook and swivel to the wire leader. If the fish appear leader-shy because the water is clear, shorten the wire leader. If they are still reluctant to bite, try a 60- or 80-pound (30 or 40 kg) monofilament leader as a last resort. But you have to work a fish fast with mono because it's no match for a "chopper's" sharp teeth.

Tripletail

Commitment is the essential key to record-fishing success, say those with multiple marks to their credit. But to what degree? To find out, I asked Captain Troy Perez, a guide of 12 years and resident of Cocoa, Florida, who has captured over 40 records—a few of which he caught with his own rod and reel—from his 18-foot (6 m) flats boat. He's had success with a variety of species, including redfish, wahoo, and amberjack, but the majority of his records are for one fish: tripletail. Why does he have so much success with this species, which looks very much like a freshwater crappie of gigantic proportions?

Captain Troy Perez knows of a perfect location for anglers who are seeking a world record on tripletail.

Here, he appears with his 20-pounder (9 kg), which he released back into Florida's water. (Courtesy Troy Perez)

"I'll go out for them every afternoon, after I finish a morning charter. The competition is stiff, so I have to fish all the time."

Also known as the "buoy fish," the tripletail has a range extending from Argentina north to Massachusetts and Bermuda in the western Atlantic Ocean. But it is most common throughout the Gulf of Mexico and on Florida's east coast near Cape Canaveral. Although the all-tackle record (42 pounds, 5 ounces [19.20 kg]) was taken in South Africa in 1989, most of the line-class records listed in the 1998 IGFA record book are from Cape Canaveral, where Perez regularly launches his boat.

Buoys are favorite hang-outs of this fish, so Perez makes his daily rounds to the two rows of bobbing objects lined up outside Port Canaveral. But he makes it his business to get to the fishing grounds first, since commercial anglers ply the waters with heavy tackle. "They get 30-pounders [13.5 kg] all the time," says Perez. "But they're using commercial gear, like 50-pound [24 kg] test. If you're out there trying to break a 6-pound [3 kg] line-class record you're going to lose a lot of fish, so you have to get more shots at them before the commercial guys show up."

Although the average tripletail in Port Canaveral weighs 12 pounds (5.4 kg), 20-pounders (9 kg) are not uncommon, which is good news for light-tackle anglers since the line class marks for both men and women are under that weight. For those targeting larger fish, Perez says tripletail get over 25 pounds (11.25 kg) here, but to find them "you better fish a lot."

His years targeting tripletail have taught him that the best time to go for trophy fish is between October and November or between May and June, when the fish are spawning. Perez likes to go out after a bad storm that's thrown a wind from the east. When everything has calmed down, an ocean swell layers grass around the buoys. He's found tripletail beneath the floating grass.

As for technique, skimmer jigs are excellent lures. Most anglers find they hook more tripletail by tipping the jig with a small piece of shrimp or squid to give it an appealing smell. That's the bait Perez—who fishes with spinning tackle—used to catch most of his records, although some anglers will use live bait, too, such as shrimp. Since this fish is wary at times, approach it with caution. Some will bring the boat just outside of casting range and place the bait or lure a few feet beyond the fish so that the retrieve will bring a hook close by the nose of the fish.

A mistake many people make is to put too much pressure on a tripletail in the beginning, says Perez. The fish will run and cut the line off against the chain beneath the buoy. "I've learned to use light pressure at first, just enough to get the fish away from the buoy."

Once you do that, says Perez, the name of the game is maximum pressure. "My advice for a record seeker is don't be afraid to lose fish. The more pressure you put on them, the better your chances of landing a record. Know the maximum limits of your drag."

Snook

In recent years, the Caribbean coast of Costa Rica has produced outstanding numbers of giant snook, including an all-tackle record of 53 pounds, 10 ounces (24.32 kg). That's not good news for anglers who are confined stateside. Still, many sportfishing veterans believe that part of the preparation required to catch record fish includes the ability to be mobile, to follow the fish.

Choosing a Travel Agent

MANY RECORD-OBSESSED anglers will tell you that the key to record-fishing success is to travel. To catch a trophy fish, you have to get to the place where the big ones are holding. To plan a fishing trip, many anglers rely on the expertise of travel agents who specialize in outdoor angling expeditions.

How do you locate a reputable agency? "Look for one with a good track record," says George Hommel Jr. of Worldwide Sportsmen, a Florida-based agency in business since 1967. Agencies in business for many years are often staffed by professionals who have traveled extensively, know the captains and crews personally, and are in constant communication with globe-trolling anglers. Three of the oldest and most respected agencies in the United States today include Frontiers International Travel, PanAngling, and Worldwide Sportsmen. Reputable agencies that specialize in fly fishing include Fishing International, the Fly Shop, and West Bank Anglers.

That's just a sampling. You can research other businesses by consulting sportfishing magazines (reputable firms often advertise), a local or national tackle shop, the IGFA or even the Internet; many of the good agencies have informative Web sites.

As you collect references, be sure to target businesses specializing in outdoor sportfishing destinations. "If you're thinking about a record fish, you don't want to book a trip through a company that deals with backpackers," says Mike Fitzgerald, co-owner of Frontiers International Travel. You can also try to locate agencies that specialize in the type of fishing you want to do. "We have clients who have been booking trips with us for over 20 years," says Fitzgerald. "Suddenly, they want to do something unusual, like go after bluefin tuna on Prince Edward Island. We don't know many charter companies in that part of the world. In that case, I'll try to locate for my client an agency that has contacts in that area."

Whatever you do, think twice before booking a trip through a local travel agent with no special expertise, one who also plans Carnival cruises for the neighbors. "If you want a serious fishing expedition, using that type of agency for anything other than airfare could be a mistake," says Fitzgerald. These professionals may not have a thorough knowledge of exotic, off-the-beaten track fishing locales. "Chances are the local agent will call me or another outdoor expert to buy a fishing package. Then they'll mark it up and sell it to you. In addition, they forward your questions to me. By the time the information gets back to you, it may be convoluted"—never mind expensive.

Some anglers will book their fishing trips directly through the charter captain or crew. If you are considering this option, keep in mind that there is an advantage to working with an agent. For record fishing, the timing of the expedition itself is very important. A crew that relies on charters to make a living may encourage you to plan a trip at the shoulder of a season when the fishing is not at its peak. By consulting an independent party, you have access to the unbiased information that can give you an advantage on the record-fishing grounds.

Jim Anson of Miami, Florida, gets around the fishing grounds by casting lines from a jonboat he trailers to various sites. This guide of five years specializes in back-country fishing for tarpon, redfish, and snook. He's put many of his clients on record fish by taking them to the action. On a recent excursion to the west coast of Florida with angler Herb Ratner, they hooked a redfish while casting lines off the edge of some mangroves. When Anson instructed Ratner to reel the fish in, the two were stunned to see a giant snook come up and eat the redfish. "That snook was 40 pounds [18 kg] or better," says Anson, who now contends that a tenacious record seeker can find his lucky snook by exploring this area, which is south of Marco Island.

In Florida, good snook fishing extends from Cape Canaveral on the east coast southward to the Florida Keys and up the west coast to Tarpon Springs. Within this range, fish that exceed 30 pounds (13.5 kg) are not uncommon, and several 40-pounders (18 kg) are caught each year. Those are the sizes both men and women need shots at to vie for one of the line-class records on this species. But count on some competition.

Perceived by many as a special fish, the snook has many fans and is ranked with bonefish and tarpon in popularity. And there is probably no saltwater fish that appeals quite as much to freshwater anglers as well, especially to bass fishermen, since the snook's basic behavior pattern is similar to that of black bass. The difference, of course, is that snook are stronger and bigger.

Found in and near many rivers, creeks, and canals that empty into salt water, this species is rarely far from some fresh or brackish water source. Mangrove shorelines are especially attractive to them, as Anson has learned, since they are structure-oriented. Snook are also found near the greatest number of forage fish. For that reason, Anson tells record hunters to use live bait. "You'll catch more snook," he says. "Try a small bait that's very active, such as pearl mullet. Snook are ambushers; they won't hit something that's just floating by."

Anson's excursions on the west coast of Florida have helped him become very intimate with the behavior of this fish. His experience has taught him that spring (April and May) can be productive there, and that snook prefer structure and will often hold on the edge of it, in a bit of shade. "They're often in the shadows, looking toward the light to see bait coming out on the tide." He's seen trophy-sized snook around jetties and rockpiles where baitfish hold. "They'll hang in the lee side of a strong tide, waiting for baitfish to come out. But the tide has to be falling pretty good."

To increase your chances of catching a snook near 40 pounds (18 kg), Anson suggests putting out two baits: a live one closer to the surface for smaller snook and another farther down for a big fish to hit, since small and big fish school together.

When it comes to record fishing, Anson takes extra steps to be prepared. Even before he gets a trophy fish on his line, he does more than just consult the IGFA book. He calls the main office and asks them about records that could be pending. "Once I get that information, I'll shoot for one that's even bigger than the pending record."

Steelhead

As you become more obsessed with your record-fishing pursuits, you'll discover that some marks require extensive research and legwork to challenge. In fact, some of the best captains and anglers have better honed investigative skills than those who call themselves professionals, including Kenneth Starr. Here's one example:

Angler and author Dave Vedder of Woodinville, Washington, is a steelhead fanatic, with *Float Fishing for Steelhead* and *Steelhead Jig Fishing* to his credit. He has also traveled extensively to fish for this native to the west coast of North America. His journeys have provided him with the insight required to target an appropriate place for trophy-sized fish. (Records for this seagoing species of rainbow trout are combined with the rainbow listings in fresh water.) The assignment is challenging because 95 percent of the steelhead rivers in the United States and Canada are catch and release, that is, any steelhead salmon that are caught must be released (hatchery-raised fish can be kept). However, Vedder has discovered one place where regulations on steelhead differ; in addition, this area regularly produces fish in the 30-pound (13.5 kg) range. (The largest line-class record to date is 31 pounds, 10 ounces [14.34 kg] on 16-pound [8 kg] test.)

The location is the Quinalt River in Washington state's Olympic National Park. Here, in protected waters, spawning grounds are in good shape. In addition, the river runs through the reservation of the Quinalt Indian tribe, where release regulations don't apply.

But there's a catch: you can only fish here when accompanied by a member of the Quinalt tribe. The good news is there are approximately 20 Quinalt guides in the area, although only a quarter of them are expert enough to tackle trophy fishing.

When packing for your trip, says Vedder, bring the lures that attract the biggest steelhead: plugs, spoons, and pink rubber worms. "One of the best spoons—the BC Steel—went out of production two years ago, but there are several good imitations on the market. The key is to find one that's silver-plated. Many of the spoons and spinners available today are nickel plated. When you put them under water, they absorb light, so fish can't see them. Very few spoons are real silver, but this metal makes a difference because it throws a lot more flash."

If you're fishing plugs, note that the best colors have proven to be various combinations of chrome and chartreuse or chrome and flame orange.

The best months to fish the Quinalt for steelhead are March and April. The ideal conditions are "when the river has been high and is dropping," says Vedder. "That could be prime time. These fish come in on high water, but they can't see a lure then because the water is muddy. When the river drops, the water clears, just as new fish—those that may have never even seen a lure before—are coming through." All of this sounds very scientific, but Vedder is quick to point out that much of it is speculation. "You can't forget that fishing is all theory."

AFTERWORD

The IGFA recently opened a special category for junior anglers. Records are now maintained for boys and girls in a "small-fry" division (through age 10) and a "junior angler" division (ages 11 through 16). IGFA started the program in January 1997 by recognizing 50 freshwater game fish and 50 saltwater species. Although junior anglers compete according to a more lenient set of rules (they don't have to kill a fish to qualify for a junior record), this new category teaches young boys and girls what it means to be sporting anglers.

"We would like to get children involved in fishing at an early age because statistics show that if they aren't introduced to fishing by the time they are teenagers, most will never take up the sport," says IGFA president Mike Leech. "Young anglers today will become constituents for preserving our fishery resources in the future. Today's young fishermen will be tomorrow's conservationists." Leech also says it's the IGFA's goal to teach junior anglers ethical fishing practices at an early age and to instill in them self confidence and a sense of pride by recognizing their outstanding angling achievements.

There is no charge to enter a potential junior world record for IGFA consideration, and anglers do not have to belong to the organization to qualify for a record. A junior membership in IGFA costs $12 ($17 international). Junior angler record application forms and a list of eligible species are available from IGFA.

IGFA's commitment to education is taking another form, too. In 1999, the

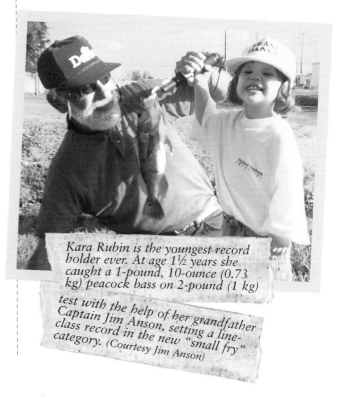

Kara Rubin is the youngest record holder ever. At age 1½ years she caught a 1-pound, 10-ounce (0.73 kg) peacock bass on 2-pound (1 kg) test with the help of her grandfather Captain Jim Anson, setting a line-class record in the new "small fry" category. (Courtesy Jim Anson)

IGFA is opening the World Fishing Center. The mission of this new headquarters is to make the name and goals of the organization more recognizable in the United States. The three-story, 60,000-square-foot facility is part of the new Sportsman's Theme Park, which includes Outdoor World, a huge sports retail center planned by Bass Pro Shops. Located in Dania, Florida, the park is just miles from the Hollywood–Fort Lauderdale Airport. IGFA's $25 million facility is expected to attract more than 500,000 visitors each year.

The idea for a fishing theme park is not unique—reputable facilities in the United States include the National Freshwater Fishing Hall of Fame in Hayward, Wisconsin, which also keeps its own records for trophy freshwater catches.

Attractions at the World Fishing Center include a research library, museum, and Fishing Hall of Fame, which features mounts of some of history's most famous record fish, including a number of the fantastic catches mentioned in this book. Displays, books, and films are complemented by lectures tailored for young people. All told, the World Fishing Center is a good place to begin an education in record fishing and respect for the resource.

For more information on the World Fishing Center, see the resources chapter.

APPENDICES

IGFA Illustrated Guide to Equipment Regulations

Double Lines and Leaders

Double lines are measured from the start of the knot, braid, roll or splice making the double to the farthermost end of the knot, splice, snap, swivel or other device used for securing the trace, leader, lure or hook to the double line. For saltwater species the double line shall be limited to 15 feet (4.57 meters) for all line classes up to and including 20 lb (10 kg); and shall be limited to 30 feet (9.14 meters) for line classes over 20 lb (10 kg). For freshwater species the double line on all classes of tackle shall not exceed 6 feet (1.82 meters).

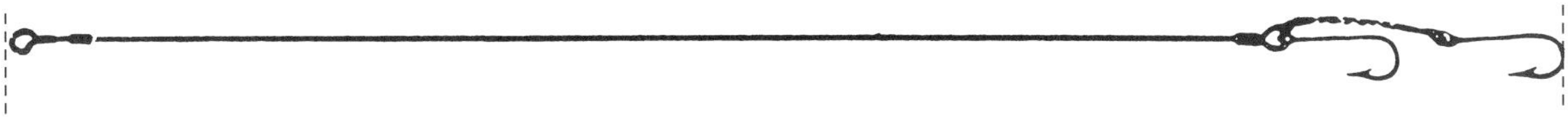

The leader shall be limited to 15 feet (4.57 meters) for saltwater species in line classes up to 20 lb (10 kg), and 30 feet (9.14 meters) for all line classes over 20 lb (10 kg). For freshwater species the leader on all classes of tackle shall be limited to 6 feet (1.82 meters).

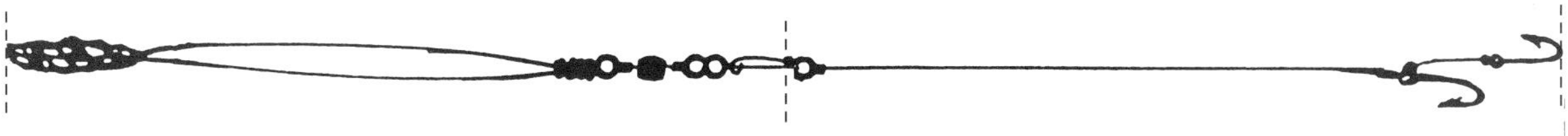

The length of the leader is the overall length including any lure, hook arrangements or other device.

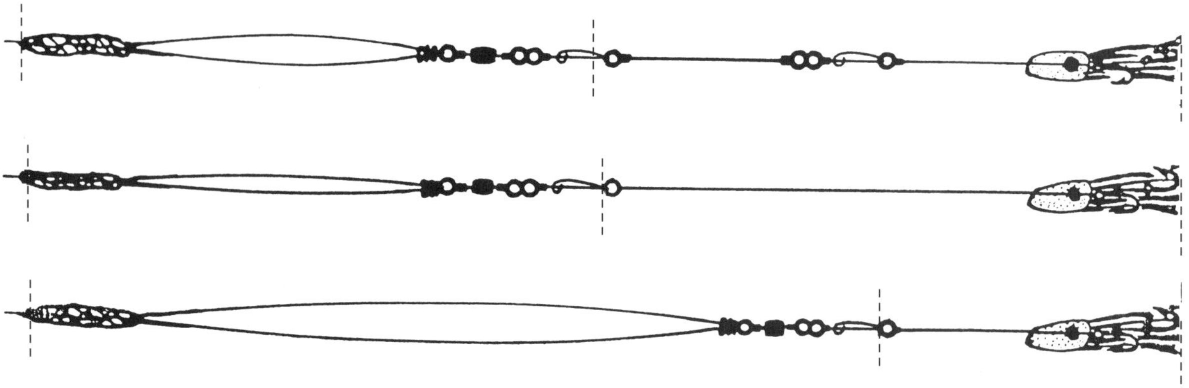

The combined length of the double line and leader shall not exceed 20 feet (6.1 meters) in line classes up to and including 20 lb (10 kg) and 40 feet (12.19 meters) in line classes over 20 lb (10 kg) for saltwater species. The combined length of the double line and leader shall not exceed 10 feet (3.04 meters) for freshwater species.

Hooks

LEGAL if eyes of hooks no more than 18 inches (45.72 cm) apart in baits and no more than 12 inches (30.45 cm) apart in lures. ILLEGAL if eyes further apart than these distances.

NOT LEGAL in bait or lures as eyes of hooks are less than hook's length (the length of the largest hook) apart.

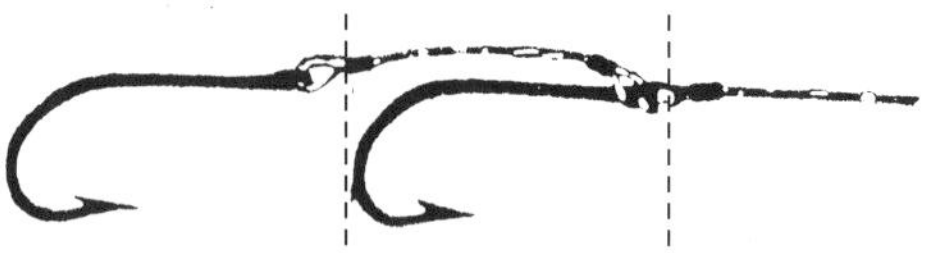

LEGAL as eyes of hooks are no less than a hook's length apart and no more than 18 inches (45.72 cm) in baits and 12 inches (30.45 cm) in lures.

LEGAL in bait and lures. The point of one hook is passed through the eye of the other hook.

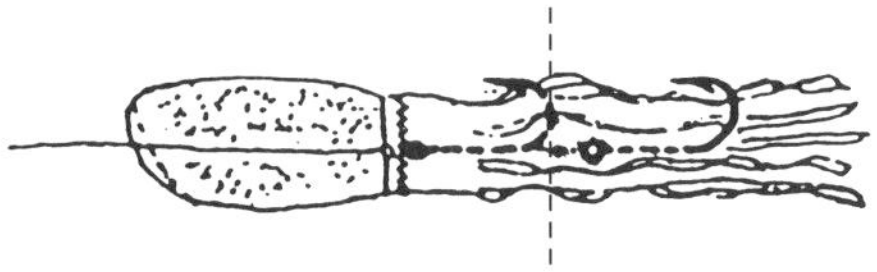

LEGAL as eyes of hooks are no less than a hook's length apart and no more than 12 inches (30.45 cm) apart, and the trailing hook does not extend more than a hook's length beyond the skirt.

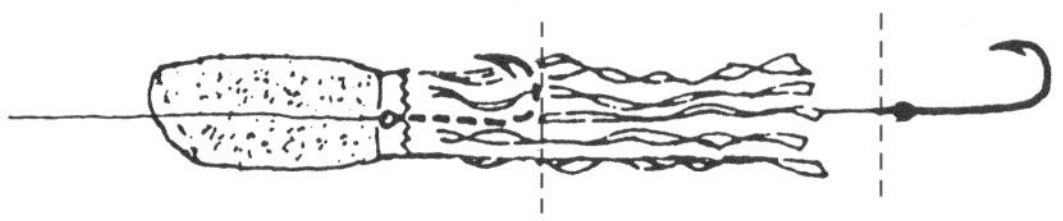

NOT LEGAL as the second or trailing hook extends more than a hook's length beyond skirt. See also two hook rigs.

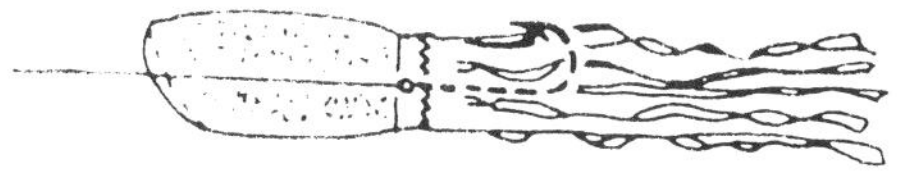

LEGAL as hook is contained within skirt.

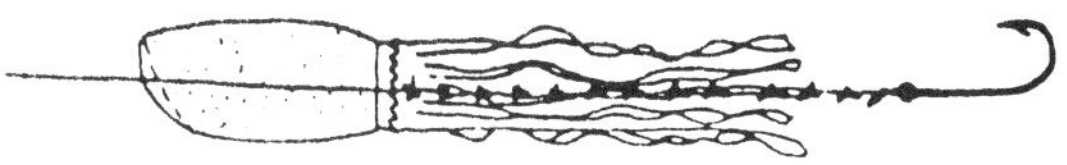

NOT LEGAL as the single hook extends more than its length beyond the skirt.

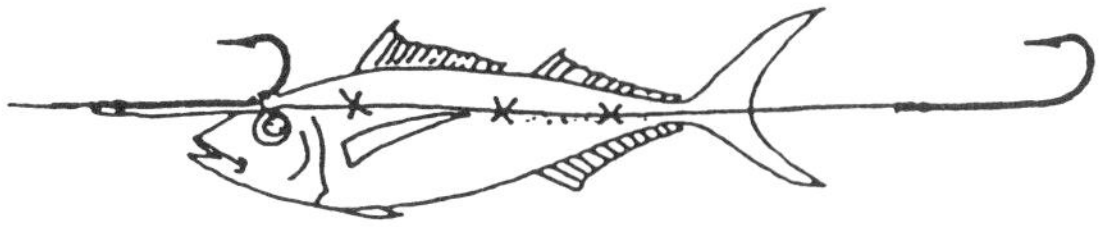

NOT LEGAL as back hook is not firmly imbedded in or securely attached to bait and is a dangling or swinging hook.

LEGAL as both hooks are firmly imbedded or securely attached to bait. Would not be legal if eyes of hooks were more than 18 inches (45.72 cm) apart.

Gaffs

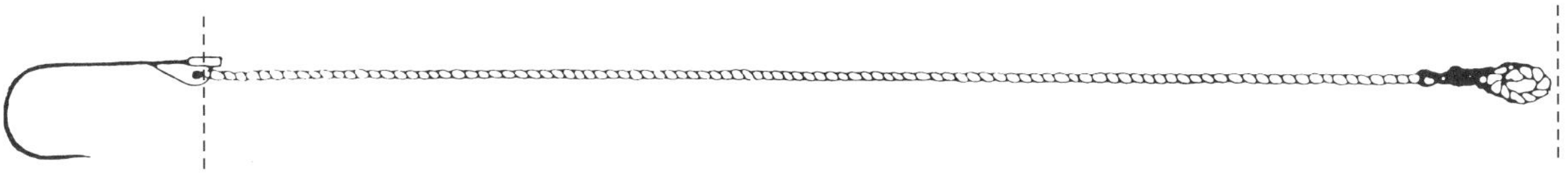

LEGAL on boats if effective length does not exceed 30 feet (9.14 meters).

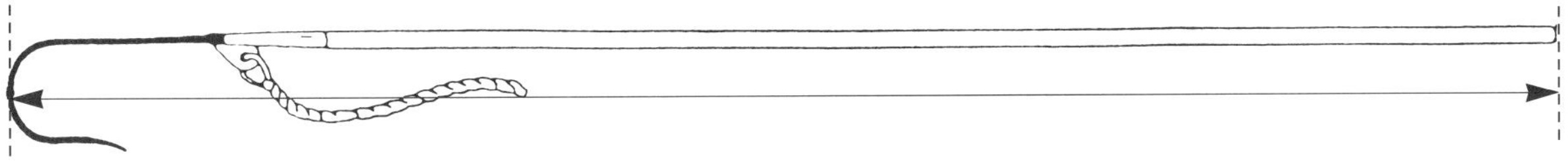

LEGAL on boats if overall length does not exceed 8 feet (2.43 meters).

IGFA World Record & Fishing Contest Application

FORM FOR RECORDING FRESHWATER & SALTWATER GAME FISH CATCHES

Read all IGFA angling rules and world record requirements before completing and signing this application. The angler's signature on the completed form must be witnessed by a notary. This application must be accompanied by line or tippet samples and photographs as specified in the World Record Requirements. Hybrids and other species which may pose a problem of identity should be examined by an ichthyologist or qualified fishery biologist.

I AM SUBMITTING THIS ENTRY FOR:

☐ An all-tackle world record.

☐ A world record in the following line class:

__________ lb/ __________ kg

☐ A fly rod world record in the following tippet class

__________ lb/ __________ kg

☐ Annual Contest ☐ Catch & Release

☐ 5-1 Club ☐ 10-1 Club ☐ 15-1 Club ☐ 20-1 Club

☐ 10 Pound Bass Club ☐ Thousand Pound Club

SPECIES

Common name: __________

Scientific name: __________

WEIGHT: Fish was weighed in ☐ lbs ☐ kgs.

lbs: __________ oz: __________ kg: ____

Digital weight (if weighed on electronic scales, give weight exactly as shown): __________

DATE OF CATCH: __________

PLACE OF CATCH: __________

____

LENGTH (See measurement diagrams)

inches: x to x __________ xx to xx__________

cm: x to x __________ xx to xx __________

GIRTH (See measurement diagrams)

inches:__________ cm: __________

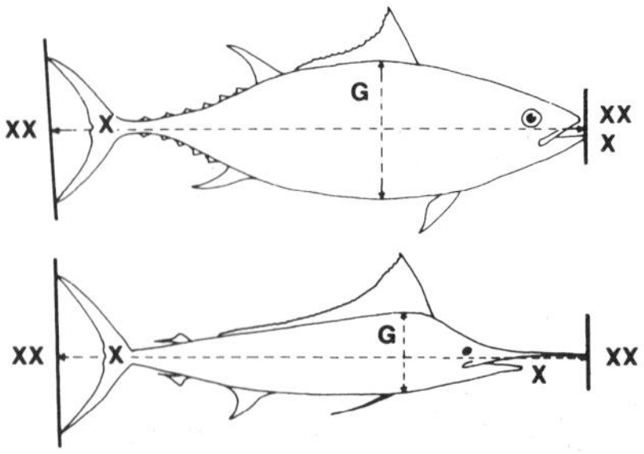

METHOD OF CATCH (trolling, casting, fly fishing, etc.):__________

FIGHTING TIME: __________

Was this catch recorded on video? __________

ANGLER (Print name as you wish it to appear on your record or contest certificate:

____

Daytime phone __________

Permanent address
(Include country and address code):

____

____

____

Age if 16 or under

Angler's fishing club affiliation (if any):

____

EQUIPMENT

Rod

Make: __________

Tip length (center of reel to end of tip): __________

Butt length (center of reel to lower end of butt):

____

Reel

Make: __________ Size __________

Line or tippet

Make:__________ Size as stated on label __________

____

☐ I am an IGFA member, enclosed is $10
☐ I am not an IGFA member, enclosed is $25
☐ Enclosed is $35 ($40 International) for membership and processing

Enclosed is $_______ check or money order for the World Record application processing fee.

Or please charge to my:

___Visa ___Mastercard ___American Express ___Discover

Account No. ☐☐☐☐☐☐☐☐☐☐☐☐☐☐☐☐

Expiration date__________Signature__________

Note: All items must be filled in. If an item does not apply, write "none used". Do not leave any spaces blank.

Length of double line: ____________________

Make of backing: ____________ Size: ________

Other equipment:

Type of gaff: __________ Length: __________

Length of trace or leader: ____________________

Number and type of hooks: ____________________

Name of lure, fly or bait: ____________________

BOAT (if used)

Name: ____________________

Make: __________ Length: __________

Captain's name: ____________________

Signature: ____________________

Address: ____________________

____

Mate's name: ____________________

Signature: ____________________

Address ____________________

____

SCALES

Location: ____________________

Type: ____________________

Manufacturer: ____________________

Date last certified: ____________________

Person and/or agency that certified scales:

____

Weighmaster: ____________________

Signature: ____________________

Address: ____________________

____

WITNESSES

Witness to weighing (other than angler, captain or weighmaster): ____________________

Address: ____________________

____

Witnesses to catch (other than captain). List two names and addresses if possible.

1. ____________________

____

2. ____________________

____

Number of persons witnessing catch: __________

VERIFICATION OF SPECIES IDENTITY
(See world record requirements.)

Signature of examining ichthyologist:

____

Title, degree, or qualifications: __________

Address: ____________________

____

Anglers are encouraged to write a detailed description of the catch and in some cases this may be required. The description may be used in a future IGFA publication.

AFFIDAVIT

I, the undersigned, hereby take oath and attest that the fish described in this application was hooked, fought, and brought to gaff by me without assistance from anyone, except as specifically provided in the regulations; and that it was caught in accordance with IGFA angling rules; and that the line submitted with this application is the actual line used to catch the fish on the stated date. I further declare that all the information in this application is true and correct to the best of my knowledge. I understand that IGFA reserves the right to employ verification procedures. I agree to be bound by any ruling of the IGFA relative to this application.

Signature of angler: ____________________

Sworn before me this __________ day of ____________________ 19______

Notary signature and seal: ____________________

When completely filled out and signed, mail this application with photos and line sample by quickest means to:

INTERNATIONAL GAME FISH ASSOCIATION, 300 Gulf Stream Way, Dania Beach, Florida 33004 USA

(This application may be reproduced.)

IGFA 10 LB BASS CLUB

Species ____________________

Weight

Fish weighed in: ❑ lbs ❑ kgs

________lbs ________oz ____________kgs

Digital weight:________ **Released: Yes**___ **No**___

Scales

Location:____________________

Type:____________________

Manufacturer:____________________

Date last certified: ____________________

Person Who Weighed Catch

Name:____________________

Address:____________________

____

Length

inches: x to x__________ xx to xx__________

cm: x to x__________ xx to xx __________

Girth

inches:__________ cm:__________

Date of Catch ____________________

Place of Catch ____________________

____

Angler

(Print name as you wish it to appear on certificate):

____

Permanent address (include country and postal code)

____

____

____

Witnesses:

Witness to weighing:____________________

Address:____________________

____

Witnesses to catch:
(Please provide name and mailing address)

1.____________________

____

____

2.____________________

____

____

Method of Catch

(trolling, casting, fly fishing, etc.):

____

Fighting Time:

____

Equipment

Rod

Make____

Tip length (center of reel to end of tip):

____

Butt length: (center of reel to lower end of butt):

____

Reel

Make:________________ Size:________________

Line or tippet

Make:____

Size as stated on label:________________ ____________

Length of trace or leader:________________________

Number and type of hooks:________________________

Name of lure, fly or bait:________________________

❑ I am a member of IGFA

❑ Please send me IGFA membership information

Boat (if used)

Name:____

Make:____

Length:____

Captain

Name:____

Address:____

____

Species Measurements:

x to x = length from lower lip to fork in tail
xx to xx = length from upper lip to point of tail
G = girth measures around fish at widest location

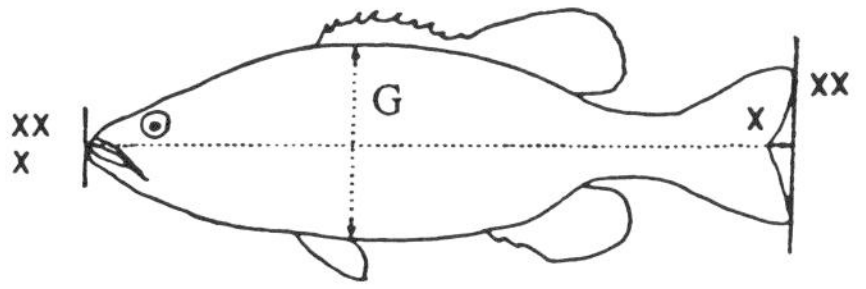

Eligible species include largemouth, smallmouth, spotted and peacock basses. All 10 lb catches, past and present are eligible as long as they can be documented and have been caught in accordance with IGFA rules. Anglers will not have to kill their bass to be eligible. Fish may be weighed in the boat, photographed and released alive. Scales should be certified for accuracy prior to the weighing or as quickly as possible after the weighing. Send completed application, photos and $25.00 registration fee to IGFA.

AFFIDAVIT

I the undersigned, hereby take oath and attest that the fish described in this application was hooked, fought, and boated by me without assistance from anyone, except as specifically provided in the regulations; and that it was caught in accordance with IGFA angling rules. I further declare that all the information in this application is true and correct to the best of my knowledge. I agree to be bound by any ruling of the IGFA relative to this application.

Signature of angler:____

Sworn before me this ______________ day of______________________________ 19__________

Notary signature and seal:____

Mail to:
International Game Fish Association
10 Pound Bass Club
300 Gulf Stream Way
Dania Beach, Florida 33004 USA
Phone (954) 927-2628

Enclosed is $25 check or money order for the 10 Pound Bass Club application processing fee. **Or please charge to my:**

___Visa ___Mastercard ___American Express ___Discover

Account No. [ ][ ][ ][ ][ ][ ][ ][ ][ ][ ][ ][ ][ ][ ][ ][ ][ ]

Expiration date________Signature________________________

RESOURCES

Books

Batin, Chris, and Terry Rudnik. *How to Catch Trophy Halibut: Proven Tips, Techniques, and Strategies of the Experts.* Fairbanks: Alaska Angler Publications, 1996.

Chapralis, Jim C. *PanAngling's World Guide to Fly Fishing.* Chicago: PanAngling, 1987.

Crabb, Bart. *The Quest for the World Record Bass.* Chicago: PanAngling, 1997.

Farrington, Chrisie. *Women Can Fish.* New York: Coward-McCann, 1951.

Fogia, Lyla. *Reel Women: The World of Women Who Fish.* New York: Three Rivers Press, 1995.

Frederiksen, Peter. *How To Catch Bluefish.* Paterson, NJ: Athletic Press, 1975.

Grey, Zane. *Tales of an Angler's El Dorado.*

International Game Fish Association. *World Record Game Fishes: 1999.* Fort Lauderdale, FL: International Game Fish Association, 1999.

Kreh, Lefty. *Fly Fishing in Salt Water.* New York: Lyons & Burford, 1986.

Marron, Eugenie. *Albacora: The Search For Giant Broadbill.* Edited by Roger Kahn. New York: Random House, 1957.

McClane, A. J. *McClane's Field Guide to Saltwater Fishes of North America: A Project of the Gamefish Research Association.* New York: Reinhart, Holt, & Wilson, 1978.

Reiger, George. *Profiles in Saltwater Angling: A History of the Sport: Its People and Places, Tackle and Techniques.* Englewood Cliffs: Prentice-Hall, 1973.

Samson, Jack. *Billfish on Fly.* Portland, OR: Frank Amato Publications, 1995.

Vedder, Dave. *Float Fishing for Steelhead: Techniques and Tackle.* Portland, OR: Frank Amato Publications, 1995.

———, and Drew Harthorn. *Steelhead Jig Fishing: Techniques and Tackle.* Portland, OR: Frank Amato Publications, 1996.

Wulff, Joan Salvato. *Joan Wulff's Fy Fishing: Expert Advice from a Woman's Perspective.* Harrisburg, PA: Stackpole Books, 1991.

MAGAZINES

Field & Stream
2 Park Avenue
New York, NY 10016
Fax 212-779-5466
http//:www.fieldandstream.com

Marlin
P.O. Box 2456
Winter Park, FL 32790

Outdoor Life
2 Park Ave.
New York, NY 10016

Sport Fishing
P.O. Box 2456
Winter Park, FL 32790

Sports Afield
250 W. 55th Street
New York, NY 10019

FISHING ORGANIZATIONS

Association of Northwest Steelheaders
P.O. Box 22065
Milwaukie, OR 97269
503-653-4176

Atlantic Salmon Federation
P.O. Box 429
St. Andrews, NB
E0G 2X0 Canada
506-529-4581
http://www.asf.ca

Bass Anglers Sportsman Society (BASS)
P.O. Box 17900
Montgomery, AL 36141
334-272-9530

Billfish Foundation
P.O. Box 8787
Fort Lauderdale, FL 33310-8787
954-938-0150
E-mail: billfish@bellsouth.net
http://www.billfish.org

Gulf Coast Conservation Association
4801 Woodway, Suite 220-W
Houston, TX 77056
713-626-4222
http://www.ccatexas.org

Federation of Fly Fishers
502 S. 19th, Suite 1
Bozeman, MT 59771-1595
406-585-7592
E-mail: 74504.2605@compuserve.com
http://www.fedflyfishers.org

Future Fisherman Foundation
1033 N. Fairfax St., Suite 200
Alexandria, VA 22314
703-519-9691

Great Lakes Sport Fishing Council
P.O. Box 297
Elmhurst, IL 60126
630-941-1351
Fax 630-941-1196
E-mail: dan@great-lakes.org
http://www.great-lakes.org

International Game Fish Association and World Fishing Center
300 Gulf Stream Way
Dania Beach, FL 33004
954-927-2628
E-mail: igfahq@aol.com
http://www.igfa.org

International Light Tackle Tournament Association
c/o Bonnie Powell
622 S. Echo Dr.
Brandon, FL 33511
813-689-2496

International Women's Fishing Association (IWFA)
P.O. Box 3125
Palm Beach, FL 33480

Muskies, Inc.
2301 7th St. N.
Fargo, ND 58102
701-239-9540

National Wildlife Federation
1400 16th St. N.W.
Washington, DC 20036-2266
202-797-6800
E-mail: action@nwf.org
http://www.nwf.org

North American Fishing Club
12301 Whitewater Dr., Suite 260
Minnetonka, MN 55343
800-843-6232
http://www.fishingclub.com

Stripers Unlimited, Inc.
P.O. Box 3045
South Attleboro, MA 02703
508-226-4007

Trout Unlimited
1500 Wilson Blvd., Suite 310
Arlington, VA 22009-2310
703-522-0200

Outfitters and Travel Booking Agencies

Anglers Travel Connections
1280 Terminal Way, Suite 30
Reno, NV 89502

Fishing International
4010 Montecito Ave.
Box 2132
Santa Rosa, CA 95405
800-950-4242
E-mail: fishint@wco.com
http://www.fishinginternational.com

Five Star Expeditions, Inc.
431 Main St.
P.O. Box 582
Lander, WY 82520

The Fly Shop
4140 Churn Creek Rd.
Redding, CA 96002
530-222-3555
Fax 530-222-3572
E-mail: info@theflyshop.com
http://www.theflyshop.com

Frontiers International Travel
100 Logan Road
P.O. Box 959
Wexford, PA 15090-0959
800-245-1950

Gateway Discount Travel
Attn: Joyce Mixon
1874 E. Main
Spartanburg, SC 29307
864-476-6354

PanAngling Travel Service
5348 W. Vermont, Suite 300A
Indianapolis, IN 46224
800-533-4353
Fax 317-227-6803
E-mail: 75037.552@compuserve.com

Rod & Reel Adventures
566 Thomson Ln.
Copperopolis, CA 95228
800-356-6982
E-mail: rod-reel@sonnet.com
http://www.rodnreeladv.com

West Bank Anglers
307-733-6483

World Wide Sportsman, Inc.
P.O. Box 787
Islamorada, FL 33036
800-327-2880
http://www.outdoor-world/wws/owrise.htm

Tag and Release Programs for Marine Fishes

Cooperative Marine Gamefish Tagging Program
NOAA/NMFS Southwest Fisheries Science Center
P.O. Box 271
La Jolla, CA 92038

Fish Unlimited Tagging Program
1 Brander Parkway
P.O. Box 1073
Shelter Island, NY 11965

Inter-American Tropical Tuna Commission
c/o Scripps Institution of Oceanography
8604 LaJolla Shores Dr.
LaJolla, CA 92037-1508

International Pacific Halibut Commission
P.O. Box 95009, University Station
Seattle, WA 98145-2009

International Sablefish Tagging Program
Alaska Fisheries Science Center
7600 Sandpoint Way NE
Bin C15700, Building 4
Seattle, WA 98115

INDEX